GLOBETROT

VISITOR'S G

# KINABALU PARK

## *Sabah, Malaysian Borneo*

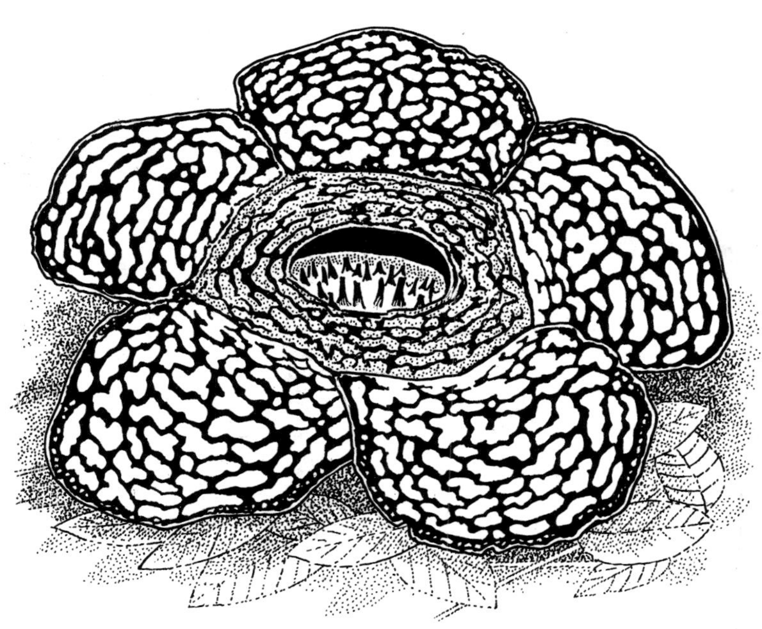

**ANTHEA PHILLIPPS**
**with**
**FRANCIS LIEW**

First published in 2000 by
New Holland Publishers (UK) Ltd
London • Cape Town • Sydney • Auckland

24 Nutford Place
London W1H 6DQ
United Kingdom

80 McKenzie Street
Cape Town 8001
South Africa

14 Aquatic Drive
Frenchs Forest, NSW 2086
Australia

218 Lake Road
Northcote
Auckland
New Zealand



2 4 6 8 10 9 7 5 3 1



ISBN 85974 405 2

**Publishing Manager**: Jo Hemmings
**Project Editor**: Mike Unwin
**Copy Editor**: Philip Cheek
**Artwork**: Michael Woods (& Mike Unwin, pp. 27, 115, 119)
**Cartographer**: Bill Smuts
**Designer**: Chris Aldridge
**Index and Proofreading**: Janet Dudley
**Production**: Joan Woodroffe

Reproduction by Modern Age Repro House Limited, Hong Kong
Printed and bound in Malaysia by Times Offset (M) Sdn Bhd

**Front Cover**: *Mount Kinabalu* (Gerald Cubitt)

# Contents

# Acknowledgements

It would not have been possible to write this guide without the assistance of many people, most of all the Park staff we have worked with over the years, in particular the Park Warden Eric Wong and the present Park Ecologist Dr Jamili Nais. The Park Rangers and Park Naturalists at the Kinabalu Park when Anthea Phillipps was Park Ecologist collaborated in many ways and she is especially grateful to the ecology section team of Tan Fui Lian, Ansow Gunsalam, Thomas Yussop, Helen Peter, Zaini Abdul Wahab, Patrick Sungkit, Dolois Sumbin, Suzanna Gangku and Hamaniah Wahab as well as to the many other park staff who assisted in research projects and field trips. We are particularly grateful to the director of the Sabah Parks Datuk Lamri Ali, for his support throughout. Ken Scriven and C.L. Chan also provided great support and encouragement.

Susan Phillipps, Quentin Phillipps, Tony Lamb and Judy Steel made invaluable comments on the text. Tom Foster and Robert New provided information on mountain-biking and the Mesilau route respectively. To them, and to all the photographers we extend our thanks. Finally, special thanks must go to Mike Unwin and Jo Hemmings at New Holland for their editorial expertise and patience.

**Photographs**

With the exception of those listed below, all the photographs in the book were taken by Gerald Cubitt.

C.L.Chan: p77 (br); p109 (tl) • Alain Compost: p59 (b); p79 (b) • Anthony Lamb: p58 (br); p91 (t); p109 (bl); p111 (t); p112 • Anthea Phillipps: p18 (b); p40 (br); p77 (bl); p80 (tr); p89; p92 (b) • C.Phillipps: p80 (b); p110 (t) • W.M.Poon: p59 (t); • Tham Yau Kong: p19 (tl); p37; p38 (b); p40 (t); p90 (t) • Chew Yen Fook: p79 (t); p90 (bl)

**SABAH TOURISM PROMOTION CORPORATION**

The publishers gratefully acknowledge the support of the Sabah Tourism Promotion Authority (SPTA) in the publication of this book. Full details of STPA are found on page 121.

# About the Authors

Anthea Phillipps was brought up in Sabah as a child, and has lived most of her life there, making many visits to Mount Kinabalu. After completing a degree in Botany at Durham University, she worked for the Sabah Museum, before joining the Sabah Parks based at Kinabalu Park headquarters in 1981. Here she worked for six years as the Park Ecologist, developing interpretation and research programmes. Her special interests centered on the rhododendrons and pitcher-plants and she is a co-author of *Rhododendrons of Sabah* and *Pitcher-plants of Borneo*, as well as an editor of the comprehensive Sabah Society publication *Kinabalu – Summit of Borneo*. Now living in Kota Kinabalu, Anthea spends her time writing, and visits the mountain whenever she can, introducing its fascinations to her two young children.

Francis Liew, BSc graduated from the University of New Brunswick, Canada in Resource Management in 1972. He joined the Sabah Parks in 1973 and served for over four years as Park Warden in charge of Kinabalu Park. He is now the Deputy Director of Sabah Parks, taking charge of the Research and Education Division. He is a keen conservationist and was instrumental in laying the foundation of the excellent park system and park management existing in Sabah today. He initiated the education and interpretation programme and also assisted in drawing up the overall park policy for Sabah.

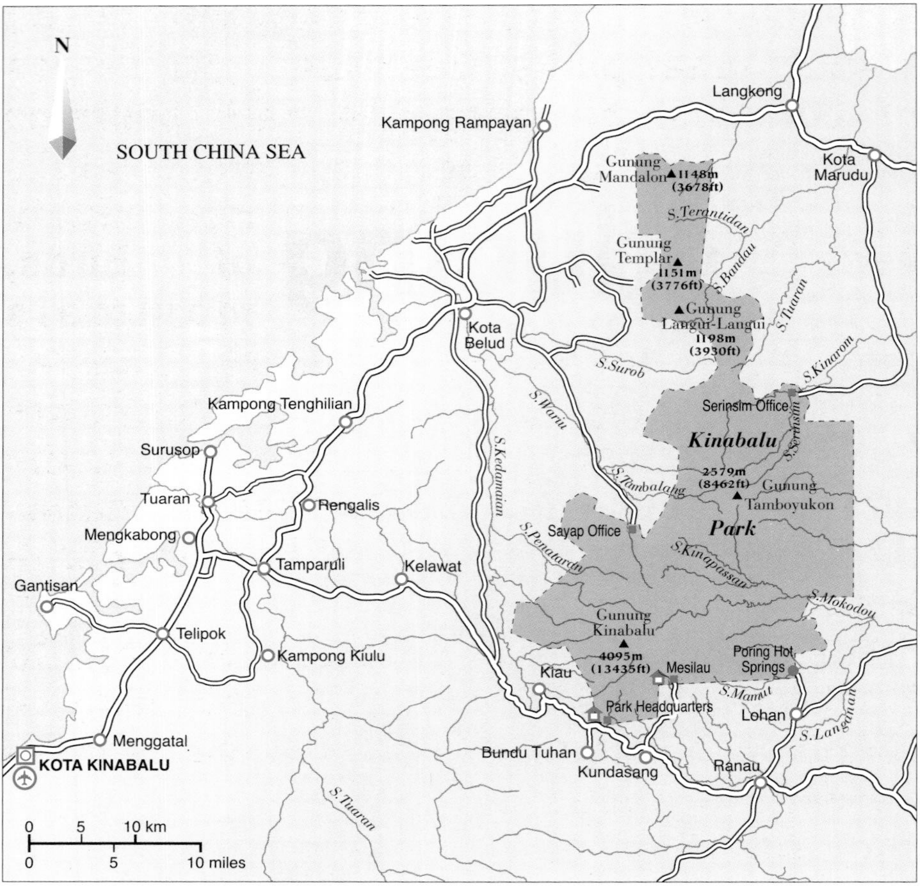

N
SOUTH CHINA SEA
Kampong Rampayan
Langkong
Kota Marudu
Gunung Mandalon
1148m (3678ft)
S.Terantidan
Gunung Templar
1151m (3776ft)
S.Bandau
Gunung Langui-Langui
1198m (3930ft)
S.Tuaran
S.Surob
S.Kinarom
Kota Belud
Kampong Tenghilian
S.Wariu
Serinsim Office
S.Serinsim
Kinabalu
2579m (8462ft)
Gunung Tamboyukon
Park
S.Kedamaian
S.Tambalang
Surusop
Tuaran
Rengalis
Mengkabong
Sayap Office
S.Penataran
S.Kinapassan
Tamparuli
Kelawat
Gantisan
S.Mokodou
Telipok
Gunung Kinabalu
4095m (13435ft)
Kampong Kiulu
Kiau
Mesilau
Poring Hot Springs
S.Mamut
Park Headquarters
Lohan
S.Langanan
Menggatal
KOTA KINABALU
Bundu Tuhan
Kundasang
Ranau
S.Tuaran
0 5 10 km
0 5 10 miles

Legend (applicable to all maps in book)
Main road
Minor road
Railway
S.Teku
Water features
City or major town
Small town or village
Gunung Kinabalu
4101m (13455ft)
Peak in metres (feet)
Campsite
Resort/lodge
Building of interest
Place of interest
Shelter
Waterfall
Cave
Airport
Bridge

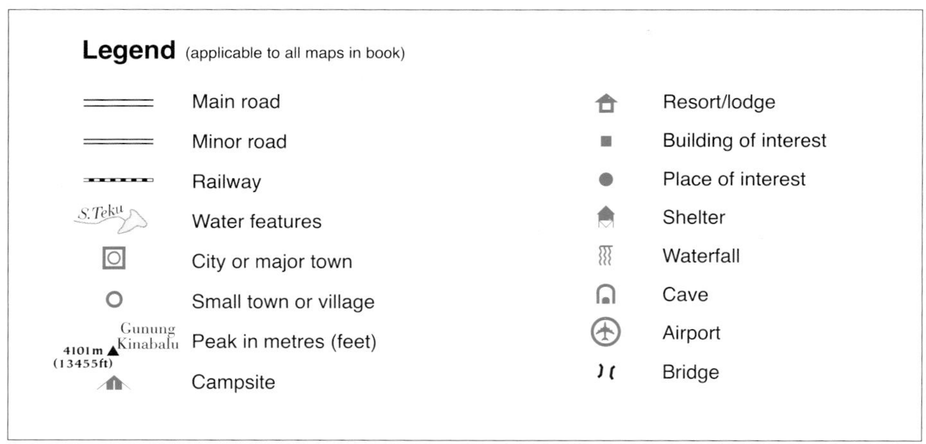

# Introducing Kinabalu

Kinabalu is, by any standards, one of the world's great parks. Described as a mecca of botanical diversity, the park contains more than 5,000 species of plants and a rich variety of birds, mammals and other animals, particularly insects, within its roughly 750 square kilometre (300 square mile) area. It is also one of the most accessible and spectacular mountains in the world, as well one of the highest in South-east Asia.

The mountain was first climbed by Sir Hugh Low in 1851, who collected many of Kinabalu's unique plants. His discoveries served to focus the attention of the scientific world on Kinabalu. Low was followed in 1888 by John Whitehead, who spent nearly two years collecting animals. Today research is directed towards the conservation of this magnificent mountain and its remarkably rich biodiversity. Established as a park in 1964, Kinabalu is now accessible to visitors who travel from around the world to experience its wonders for themselves.

# Summit of Borneo

Kinabalu is situated in the East Malaysian state of Sabah on the island of Borneo. Politically Borneo is divided into four parts. The biggest south-eastern portion (Kalimantan) belongs to Indonesia. Sarawak on the west coast and Sabah to the north form the East Malaysian states within the federation of Malaysia, with the tiny oil-rich independent sultanate of Brunei Darussalam tucked in between.

## GEOGRAPHY, GEOLOGY AND CLIMATE

Kinabalu is basically a huge granite dome that was pushed up through the earth's crust as molten rock millions of years ago. The accompanying upheavals, foldings and faultings formed the surrounding sedimentary shales and sandstones into the nearby mountain ranges of Crocker and Trus Madi. Geologically, Kinabalu is a very young mountain. The granite cooled and hardened only about 10 million years ago and today is said to be still rising at the rate of about 5 millimetres (1/5 inch) a year.

During the ice ages about 100,000 years ago, the mountain was covered by a huge sheet of ice and gigantic glaciers flowed down its slopes, scouring the surface. Only the sharp summit peaks stood out above the ice. One such glacier exploited a line of weakness to the north, spilling into the chasm of Low's Gully, more than 1,800 metres (6,000 feet) down and splitting the mountain into two arms, forming the western and eastern summit plateaux. Legends were told of a great lake on top of the mountain which never existed in reality, but which may have its basis in folk memory of this shining sheet of ice, with sharp peaks jutting above like islands.

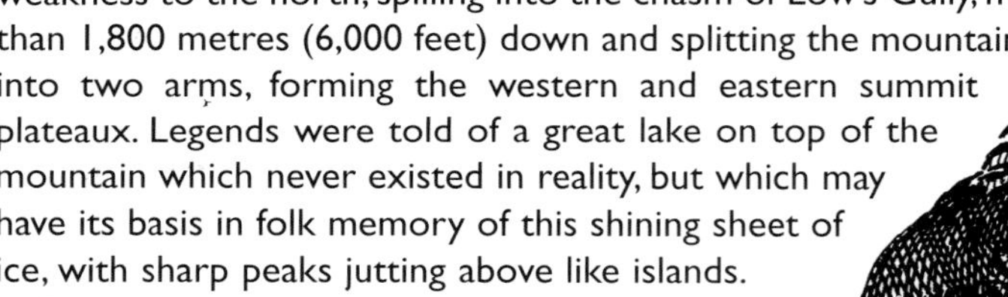

The icecap is thought to have melted about 3,000 years ago, but the glacier-smoothed slopes of the summit plateau and the jagged ice-plucked peaks bear mute witness to its frozen past. Today wind and rain continue the erosion process and large slabs of granite flake off the surface in a process known as exfoliation, caused by alternating high and low temperatures. Clusters of small circular pits in the rock slabs, a few centimetres deep, are the result of continuing frost action. Other features visitors notice on the summit plateau are long white rock bands or dykes that intruded through cracks in the

*Kinabalu Serpent-eagle*

granite massif as it rose. Today no snow falls on the mountain, though there are rare reports of ice forming in the little rock pool at the summit. This is the 'sacrificial pool' or 'wishing pool', so called because in the early days it was a traditional site for offerings to the mountain spirits.

**How high?**

Most guidebooks published before 1997 will give the height of Kinabalu as 4,101 metres (13,455 feet). A re-survey carried out in 1997, using satellite technology, removed several metres from the summit, cutting it down to 4,095 metres (13,435 feet), but Kinabalu still retains its title as the highest mountain between Wilhelmina in Irian Jaya (4,509 metres/14,793 feet) and the mighty snow-capped Himalayas.

Because of the mountain's relative youth, the terrain is steep and precipitous with knife-edge ridges. Landslides are common. Rainfall is high and often torrential, with an average of about 2,700 millimetres (110 inches) a year recorded at the Park HQ (1,563 metres/5,128 feet), around 3,300 millimetres (130 inches) at Panar Laban (3,270 metres/10,728 feet), and about 2,500 millimetres (130 inches) at the Poring Hot Springs (550 metres/1,805 feet). Waterfalls are many. The long scarf-like Kadamaian waterfall on the southern flank of the mountain is one of the most spectacular in wet weather, when sheets of rain slide across the summit plateau and pour down its sides. This waterfall is easily seen from the road, about 10 minutes from the Park Headquarters entrance, if the weather is fine.

The Park is affected by both the south-west monsoon from May to July and by the north-east monsoon from November to January, which are the wettest months. The driest time is usually in March and April. The period between the monsoons in August and September is also usually fairly dry but climatic variations can occur in any year. Severe droughts during major El Nino events affected the mountain in 1973, 1983, 1992 and most recently in 1998. During the 1998 El Nino event only 31 millimetres (1¼ inches) of rain were recorded at Park HQ between January and April, in comparison to around 850 millimetres (33 inches), during a normal year. Large numbers of dead trees killed by the drought can still be seen on several parts of the mountain.

## HISTORY

Today's relatively comfortable two day climb to the summit is a far cry from the travails of the early explorers. In 1851, Sir Hugh Low, credited as the first person to climb the mountain, took nine days to reach the summit plateau, travelling in a party of 42 people.

Low and Whitehead both started their historic ascents from the village of Kiau, situated on the southern flank of the mountain near the Kadamaian waterfall and recruited their guides and porters here. This route was both steep and arduous, and when the park was gazetted in 1964 and the HQ was established, the ascent route was changed to the present one. People from the nearer village of Bundu Tuhan supplied most of the guides and porters, and Bundu Tuhan's most famous son, Gunting bin Lagadan, reputed to possess remarkable powers, became the first officially registered park guide.

Low, then the Colonial Secretary for the British crown colony of Labuan, was intensely interested in plants, coming as he did from a long line of horticulturalists in England. He was so astonished by the richness of the plant life he saw on his first journey, that he climbed the mountain twice more, both times with his good friend Spenser St. John, the British Consul in Brunei, in April and again in July in 1858. Several of Kinabalu's most spectacular species were later named after Low, including the most bizarre pitcher plant, the largest rhododendron, and the dainty mountain buttercup. Though Low reached the summit plateau, he did not reach the peak that now bears his name. That honour was left to John Whitehead, a zoologist who discovered two of Kinabalu's most spectacular birds, Whitehead's Trogon and Whitehead's Broadbill. After several months collecting on the mountain in 1888 he finally reached the summit in the same year.

Low's discoveries focused the attention of the scientific world on Kinabalu, but it was not until 1910 that the first botanist (and incidentally the first lady), Lilian Gibbs, climbed the mountain and discovered many species new to science. Increasing interest in the mountain's natural riches culminated in major expeditions organised by the Royal Society of Great Britain in 1961 and 1964. Both were led by the eminent tropical botanist Prof E.J.H.Corner, who made it clear in his report on the 1961 expedition to the government of British North Borneo (as Sabah was then called), that the mountain's plant and animal life were of exceptional interest.

Thus it was that in 1964 the Kinabalu Park was finally gazetted, covering an area of approximately 711 square kilometres (274 square miles). Over the years the boundaries have changed from time to time and today the Park covers a total of some 753 square kilometres (291 square miles).

When the park first opened it was a far cry from the world class facility is is today. In the early years the road to the park was largely a narrow muddy earth track, passable only to 4-wheel drive vehicles. This restricted access to real enthusiasts, but when the road was finally sealed in 1981 visitor figures shot up. Today more than 200,000 people visit the park each year. Most visitors to the park in the past came either to climb the standard trail to the summit or to wonder at the rich diversity of the plants. Within the last few years however, an increasing number have come to enjoy more strenuous activities, including mountain running and mountain bike races described in detail on pages 32–33.

## THE DUSUN PEOPLE

The slopes of Kinabalu are inhabited by the local Dusun people, hill farmers who practise shifting cultivation. Traditional crops such as hill rice, tapioca and sweet potatoes are still grown extensively, but in the 1950s the introduction of temperate vegetable farming was started and changed the way of life for many. By 1958 the government-approved list of vegetables included cabbages, carrots, french beans, celery, capsicums and tomatoes. Today roses, chrysanthemums and other cut flowers are also grown.

Hill farming is still practised, the main crops now being rice and pineapples – the roadside stalls at the small town of Kundasang, six kilometres (ten miles) beyond

Park HQ are daily loaded down with local produce. The Kinabalu Park and the tourist industry are also major employers, and the sale of handicrafts and souvenirs has also become a popular source of income for local people.

Many of the plants within and around the edges of the Park are still used by the Dusun for medicine, food, fuel, construction and handicrafts. In 1992 the Kinabalu Ethnobotanical Project was started by the Park staff. The purpose of this was to collate information on the plants used by the Dusun people. By 1998, when the project was wound down, more than 9,000 specimens had been collected. The results show that traditional medicine is still the main recourse for many people who fall sick, with 31% of the plants recorded being used in this way.

## Dusun beliefs

An ancient mythology lies at the heart of Dusun culture. A Dusun creation myth tells how the supreme deities Kinohoringan and his wife Umunsumundu created the universe. Umunsumundu made the earth while Kinohoringan created the sky and the clouds. But the clouds were smaller than the earth and Kinohoringan was ashamed. To save his pride, Umunsumundu reshaped the earth, making it smaller, and thus created Kinabalu, the mountain that we know today.

The mountain has always been central to the lives of the Dusun and for centuries they believed the summit to be the home of their departed spirits and considered the mountain to be sacred. Low, Whitehead and others had to follow various rituals to appease the mountain spirits at several places on the ascent, involving sacrificial offerings of chickens, eggs and tobacco. Taboos during the climb used to include no throwing of stones or making of unnecessary noise.

Even the name Kinabalu is now thought to derive from the Dusun words for a big boulder associated with spirits. The early explorers were fascinated by its origins and wove tales and legends of their own out of them, involving dragons, widows, pearls and Chinese princes. Sometimes, when swirling clouds deaden any sound in the misty forest, the presence of spirits seems very close and they pervade the stories and legends of Kinabalu.

A Dusun story tells of a giant king named *Gayo Nakan* ('big eater') who lived at the base of the mountain. His people tired of his enormous appetite and were hard pressed to feed him. Hearing their complaints, the king told them to bury him alive at the top of the mountain. Bringing all their tools they laboured in vain, until the king uttered magic words and sank into the rock up to his shoulders. He then told his people that, due to their lack of patience, drought and famine would afflict them – but promised to help them in times of war. Fearful and penitent, the people made the first sacrificial offerings at the wishing pool below the summit that was *Gayo Nakan's* grave.

Today many of the younger Dusun people have mixed feelings about these beliefs, but the ritual sacrifice of seven white chickens is still performed once a year at Panar Laban to invoke blessings on the mountain climbers.

## Essential facts

**LOCATION:** Situated some 80kms (50 miles) from Sabah's capital of Kota Kinabalu on Sabah's west coast and covers an area of 753 sq. kms (291 sq. miles). The elevation of the park ranges from 150m (492 feet) in the lowlands at Serinsim, to the summit of Mount Kinabalu at 4,095m (13,435 feet).

**CLIMATE:** Average temperatures range from 15°C–24°C (60°–78°F) at Park HQ at 1,563m (5128 feet), where it can be quite hot during the day but much cooler at night. Poring Hot Springs at 550m (1,804 feet) in the lowlands ranges from 20°C–32°C (70°–94°F) and is hot and humid during the day but cool at night. At Panar Laban Resthouse at 3,270m (10, 728 feet) on the summit trail, average temperatures vary from 6°C–14°C (42°–58°F), but can sometimes reach almost freezing at night.

**WHEN TO GO:** The best time to visit Kinabalu is during the dry season from February to April, when walking and climbing is much more enjoyable. Dryer periods of several days also often occur in the inter-monsoon season, between August and September.

**ACCESS:** The Kinabalu Park HQ is the main entry point for most visitors and is only two hours drive from KK on a good sealed road. Poring is another major entry point, an hour's drive beyond park HQ, also on a sealed road.

**PERMITS:** Permits and guides are compulsory for the summit trail and for all climbing routes, including the Gunung Namboyukon trail at Serinsim, and for any area of the park not part of the normal trails. Entry fees are payable at Park HQ and at Poring Hot Springs unless accommodation is prior booked. Fees are payable for the Mountain Garden at Park HQ, the *Nepenthes Rajah* Trail at Mesilau and the Canopy Walkway, Butterfly Farm, Orchid Centre and Tropical Garden at Poring Hot Springs, and for guided walks.

**EQUIPMENT:** Camping equipment can be hired at Poring only. Climbers and mountain bikers should bring their own equipment. Insect repellent and good walking shoes or trainers are essential, as well as a pair of rubber sandals. Leech socks and a swimsuit are useful for the lowland forest. Trail walkers and climbers should bring a daypack, a water bottle, a rain coat, a good supply of plastic bags, and a warm jacket for nights. Mountain climbers should bring warm, waterproof clothing, as well as a torch, hat and gloves. Sunscreen and sunglasses are useful.

**FACILITIES:** Park HQ has chalets, hostels, restaurants, an interpretation centre, a conference hall, a fitness centre and souvenir shops. Poring has chalets, hostels, a camp ground, souvenir shop, hot sulphur water pools, swimming pools, a butterfly farm, orchid conservation centre, tropical garden and canopy walkway. The Mesilau resort has chalets, hostels, reception centre, restaurant and interpretation centre. Sayap has no faciliites, but camping is permitted on flat ground near the staff quarters. Serinsim has no facilities apart from a public toilet and a covered cooking/eating area by the river where visitors may camp.

# Planning and Practicalities

Malaysia as a whole is one of the most accessible Asian destinations for the overseas traveller. The simplest way to visit Kinabalu is on an organised tour, but such tours do not always leave enough time to soak up the atmosphere of the mountain. All tour agencies in Kota Kinabalu will arrange stays in the Park on a group or individual basis, as well as transport to and from Park Headquarters, Mesilau and Poring, but it is not hard to do it yourself. Accommodation can be booked by phone but you should visit the Kinabalu Nature Resort office in Kota Kinabalu in person to pay for it if you have not made arrangements through an agency. Hiring your own vehicle is the only way to reach Sayap and Serinsim, which are seldom on tour itineraries. Most people speak at least some English. All major roads are well signposted and if you do get lost, you will generally find people are friendly and helpful. Remember to drive on the left.

# Getting There

## WHEN TO GO

Borneo has a tropical climate with an average daily temperature around 32°C (90°F) and a relative humidity between 85 and 95%. In the mountains it can still be quite hot during the day, but is considerably cooler at night when temperatures at the Kinabalu Park HQ and Mesilau can drop to 15°C (60°F). In Sabah the main rainy seasons are from November to January when the rains come with the north east monsoon, and from May to July, with the south west monsoon. Mornings are usually clear at any season. Sabah lies below the typhoon belt, though the tail-ends can cause strong winds and rain during the typhoon season. On Kinabalu, the driest time of the year is usually between February and April, but seasonal variations can occur in any year.

## HOW TO GET THERE

Most overseas visitors will arrive in Malaysia by plane. The standard route to Kinabalu is by air, via Kuala Lumpur in Peninsular Malaysia, to Kota Kinabalu in Sabah, and then onwards to the park overland.

### Kuala Lumpur/Peninsular Malaysia

Major airlines fly into Kuala Lumpur, the capital of Malaysia. The new RM9 billion Kuala Lumpur International airport (KLIA) at Sepang in West (Peninsular) Malaysia is an ultra-modern and welcoming sight after a long flight. There are about 36 international carriers servicing the airport. The arrivals procedure is straightforward and signs (in Bahasa Malaysia and English) are self-explanatory.

### Kota Kinabalu/Sabah

Passengers continuing on to Kota Kinabalu, the capital of the state of Sabah, have to change flights here. Kota Kinabalu can also be reached by direct flights from Singapore, Hong Kong, Manila, Brunei and Taipei.

### Park Headquarters

From Kota Kinabalu (KK), local buses run once a day to Ranau from the main outstation bus stop in town, passing the entrance to the Park HQ on the way. The buses leave KK at around 7.00 a.m. reaching the Park HQ at about 9.00 a.m. To return to KK simply sit and wait at the bus stop on the main road outside the entrance before 9.00 a.m., and take any bus going to KK. Getting a bus later in the day may be more difficult.

Car rentals can be arranged through major hotels in KK. At the time of writing, taxis to Ranau charge RM 75.00 per person to Park HQ and take a maximum of four passengers. They leave from the same outstation bus stop before 8.00 a.m. You can nogotiate for the taxi to pick you up from Park HQ for your return if you hire the whole taxi.

### Poring Hot Springs

If you do not have your own transport it is best to arrange this once you reach the Kinabalu Park HQ, through the Sabah Parks or the accommodation management, Kinabalu Nature Resort. You could also get a bus to Ranau, where you change to the minibus to Poring.

### Sayap and Serinsim

A 4-wheel drive vehicle is essential for these destinations.

## The Ringgit

The Malaysian currency is known as the Ringgit (RM) and there are 100 sen to each Ringgit. Notes come in denominations of RM 2, RM 5, RM 10, RM 20, RM 50 and RM 100. There are coins of the following denominations: 1, 5, 10, 20, 50 sen and RM 1.

### Mesilau

If the unsealed stretch of road between Kundasang and Mesilau has been graded recently it is possible to do this trip in an ordinary car but a 4-wheel drive is always advisable. Transport can be arranged through Kinabalu Gold and/or Sabah Parks at Park HQ.

### Immigration, Visas and Customs

All visitors to Malaysia require a valid passport and must complete a Disembarkation Card, which is printed in English. Most visitors are granted a two month visa-free stay upon arrival; however, this is best confirmed by the nearest Malaysian Embassy prior to travel to Malaysia.

Once in the country, visa extensions may be sought from the nearest Immigration Office, especially in Kota Kinabalu.

Certain items (e.g. taped videos) need to be declared at the Customs counters but there are no declaration forms to complete apart from a recently introduced Traveller's Currency Declaration Form (see **Currency** below). All plant derivatives must also be declared to the Plant Quarantine Office.

**Drugs are taken very seriously by the Malaysian authorities, and those convicted of drug trafficking can face the death penalty.**

If entering the country through KL, you must also pass through Sabah immigration on arrival (as do passengers direct from Singapore, Hong Kong, etc).

### Currency and Credit Cards

The Malaysian currency is known as the Ringgit (RM). Asian exchange rates have varied greatly over the past few years and the following should be used as a guide only: RM 3.8 to 1$US, RM 6.00 to 1Pound Sterling, RM 2.4 to 1$ Aust..

It is best to change money in KK, prior to departure for the park, at any major-bank or money changer. Recent currency controls restrict the flow of currency into and out of the country. Foreigners and non-residents are allowed to carry not more than RM 1000 and an unlimited amount of foreign currency when entering or leaving the country. However, the amount declared upon departure cannot exceed that declared when entering the country.

Major credit cards (Visa, Mastercard, Diners and Amex) are accepted at most larger establishments in KK, but visitors should bring enough cash for food and sundry items purchased at the park outlets. Travellers' cheques are best changed in KK.

Tipping is not essential, though in big establishments a 10% service charge may be incorporated into the final bill. However, small change is normally left and those who offer exceptional service are usually rewarded.

**Health**

Malaysia is actually a very healthy country. If visiting Poring overnight or Sayap or Serinsim, malarial precautions are advisable but are not necessary for Kota Kinabalu or for the Park HQ and Mesilau. Leeches occur in some lowland areas, mainly in the forest around Poring . Prevention is best – wear proper boots or walking shoes with 2 pairs of long knee socks or a pair of leech socks, and spray both shoes and socks with inspect repellent. If you do get bitten apply salt or a lighted cigarette to remove the leech if you don't want to pull it off, and put a small plaster over the cut. Most septic bites are caused by secondary infections, so don't scratch a healing bite. Anti-histamine cream will deal with most insect bites and is widely available from pharmacies in KK. Panadol, plasters and an antiseptic cream are also useful, as is a pair of tweezers for removing thorns. In the lowlands those who are not used to the heat will sweat a lot and must take care to replenish body fluid to avoid dehydration. If you use any kind of medication regularly it is advisable to bring an ample supply with you as you may not be able to get the same drugs in Sabah.

If you plan to climb Kinabalu and have any kind of medical condition, please get your doctor's advice first. This is particularly important if you suffer from asthma, diabetes, high blood pressure, heart or lung problems. Though it can be very cold on the summit plateau, if it is a clear day it can also be very hot – sunblock cream and a sunhat are useful under such conditions. It is not unknown for climbers to suffer heatstroke after a whole day on the summit plateau under clear skies. Many people suffer from headaches, nausea or disorientation due to mild altitude

## What to bring

The following items will help make your visit more enjoyable:

- swimwear
- lightweight clothing
- walking shoes
- raincape
- hat
- gloves
- rubber sandals
- ziploc plastic bags
- leech socks
- warm jacket
- lightweight rucksack
- day pack
- sunscreen
- insect repellent
- water bottle
- torch and batteries
- camera (with plenty of film, spare battery, and flash)
- reading materials (entertainment is limited)
- basic first aid kit
- this guidebook

THE MASSIVE ROCK BUTTRESS OF KINABALU DOMINATES THE LANDSCAPE OF NORTHERN SABAH.

ABOVE: THE LOCAL PEOPLE HAVE LIVED AROUND THE MOUNTAIN FOR CENTURIES, FARMING ITS LOWER SLOPES.

ABOVE RIGHT: AT KOTA BELUD NEAR THE PARK, LOCAL FARMERS BRING THEIR PRODUCE TO MARKET.

RIGHT: AT NEARLY 3500 METRES LABAN RATA RESTHOUSE AT PANAR LABAN OFFERS HIGH ALTITUDE COMFORT.

OPPOSITE BELOW: PANAR LABAN ALSO HAS MORE BASIC OVERNIGHT ACCOMMODATION FOR THOSE HEADING FOR THE SUMMIT.

OPPOSITE ABOVE: AT PARK HEADQUARTERS, VISITORS CAN ENJOY A FULL RANGE OF AMMENITIES.

TOWERING OVER 3900 METRES (12,800 FEET), SOUTH PEAK IS A FORBIDDING SPECTACLE OF BARE ROCK.

sickness at the overnight hostel at Panar Laban (3,262 metres/10,703 feet). Headache tablets and anti-nausea medications such as dramamine may help, but if symptoms are severe do not continue the climb.

All the park staff are trained in basic mountain rescue and first aid. In a major medical emergency, the nearest district hospital is in Ranau; the staff there will tranfer serious cases to the government hospital in KK, usually by road. There are private medical clinics in Ranau as well and a well-equipped private hospital, the Sabah Medical Centre, in KK.

**Equipment**

The best advice when planning a trip to places such as Kinabalu is to use your common sense. Take sensible clothing and avoid weighing yourself down with unnecessary items. Kinabalu can be climbed in sensible walking shoes, but make sure these are in good repair or take a spare pair as well. Take an umbrella or buy one on arrival. Rain can often come on suddenly, even in the dry season, and raincoats are too hot in the lowland forests such as those around Poring, though they are essential higher up the mountain.

Bear in mind that most supplies can be bought in Kota Kinabalu while even small sundry shops further afield will usually sell bottled water, matches, candles and mosquito coils as well as basic food supplies. A good supply of plastic bags of various sizes is always useful as is a penknife, masking tape, needles and thread, plasters and headache tablets.

For the mountain climb, bring a complete change of clothes, raincoat or umbrella (umbrellas often usefully double as walking sticks), warm jersey and/or jacket, gloves, woolly hat, sunhat, sunblock cream, sunglasses, spare pair of shoes or rubber sandals to change into at the hostel if the pair you are wearing get soaked, chocolate, raisins etc., water bottle, camera, film, toilet paper or tissues, a small torch and spare batteries. If your rucksack is not waterproof, pack everything in double plastic bags in case of rain. Sleeping bags and/or blankets are provided at the hostels.

For Poring Hot Springs take a towel, swimsuit and plenty of insect repellent for your skin - as well as insect spray for your shoes and socks and to kill any ants that may have invaded the chalets. Mosquito coils are also useful, but both these and insect spray can be bought on arrival in KK. For walking in the forest at any altitude, long trousers tucked into your socks and a long-sleeved shirt offer most protection. Sensible walking shoes are essential.

Few tourists these days travel without a still or video camera. It is wise to be well equipped, however carrying too much can be a nuisance, so getting the right balance is important. While there is a loss in picture quality with many zoom lenses, they do save on weight. Longer lenses (e.g. 200mm) are good for taking wildlife, people and distance shots. A small tripod is useful in low light situations inside the rainforest or caves. Alternatively, take a flash and/or fast film. A polarising filter can be helpful, and for overcast skies graduated blue and yellow filters are useful. Photographers can get most types of commonly used films and batteries in photographic shops in KK, but choices may be more limited elsewhere. Bring spare batteries as they and other equipment are not always available in the park. Choosing slide or print film depends upon how the photographs will be used and who will see them. It is expensive to obtain prints from slides but almost impossible to get good slides from prints. Whilst print film is readily available, slide film is more scarce. Photographers are generally advised to bring their own film.

**Local Time**

All parts of Malaysia are in the same time zone. This is 8 hours ahead of GMT all year around.

**Electricity**

Electricity is available in all but the most isolated villages in Sabah. The system is 240-volt 50-cycle. For those with equipment that operates on a different system, adapters are often available, though if in doubt it is best to bring your own. Electricity is provided around the clock at all park outlets except Sayap and Serinsim, where generators are switched on for a few hours in the morning and evening.

**Water**

Water from hotels in KK is generally safe to drink, but in the park visitors are best advised to take bottled mineral water or to boil everything they drink. Drinking from streams along the trails should be avoided.

**Language**

The official language in Malaysia is Bahasa Malaysia, although many Malaysians speak several languages and will use them all in general conversation. The language is similar to that spoken by some people in

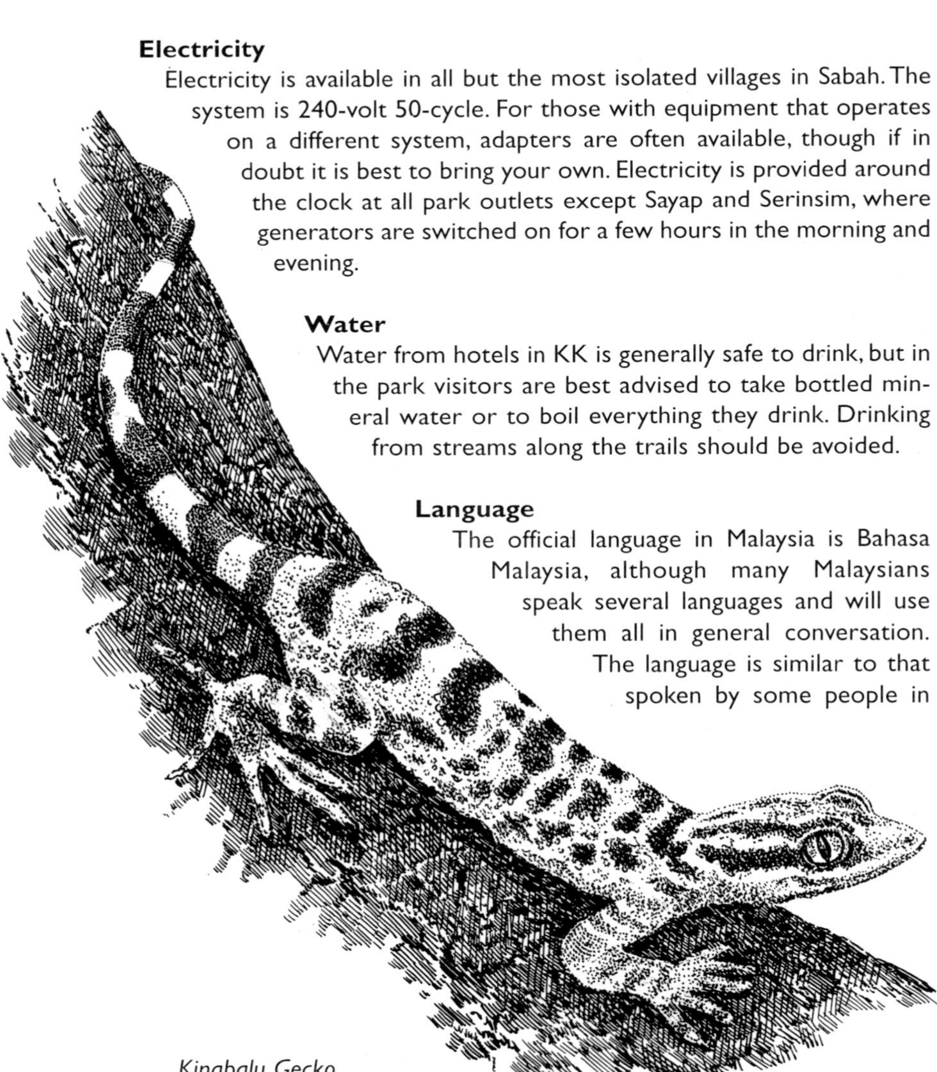

*Kinabalu Gecko*

southern Thailand and those in Indonesia, Brunei and parts of the island of Mindanao in the Philippines. Several Chinese dialects are also spoken widely in Sabah.

English is a compulsory subject in all schools and is widely understood, especially in the main towns and by tour operators and guides. Many words have been adapted from English, so English speaking tourists will often notice phrases they can understand.

Borneo's large number of ethnic peoples has resulted in over 20 major native dialects being spoken in Sabah. Around Kinabalu most local people are from the Dusun tribes. All but the elderly will speak Malay as well as Dusun, and most will also speak some English. People in Sabah are almost invariably friendly and polite. Follow their example. Shouting in public if things go wrong is viewed as very bad manners, whereas a quiet request to speak to someone more senior will often get results.

### Communications

Malaysia is well connected to terrestrial, satellite and cyberspace communications networks. Public phones accept either coins or prepaid phonecards that can be purchased from stores that display the sign '*Kadfon*'. Cards are sold by Telekom Malaysia and various private operators. Local, domestic and international telephone calls may be made from Park Headquarters and Mesilau, but not from Poring.

### Safety

Malaysia is a relatively safe country to travel through, with few physical threats. Most of the reported crime appears to be petty, with robberies and snatchings about all a visitor may encounter. Travellers therefore need not be unduly anxious, but should take the usual precautions such as keeping separate records of travel documents, traveller's cheques and credit cards. A concealed money pouch is advisable but not essential. Visitors should take care in areas where pickpockets operate, such as crowded bus stations, shopping malls and markets.

Travel insurance is always wise in case of theft, illness or other problems. The cost and degree of cover provided by such policies varies greatly so it is advisable to check before purchasing such insurance – for example expensive items like cameras may have limited cover.

### Women Travelling Alone

Most women should not be threatened by travelling alone or with others in Malaysia, as long as they dress appropriately. Tight or revealing clothing can be seen as suggestive. Some Malaysians may ask whether single women are married and/or whether they have a boyfriend – more out of curiosity than anything else. It is probably best to dismiss any such enquiries with a friendly smile. Single women should take the same safety measures as other travellers (see **Safety** above).

### Shopping

In KK the main shopping centres are open daily from 10.00 – 20.00, sometimes later. Smaller shops often open at 8.00 or 9.00 and close earlier. Markets, especially food markets, are popular in the early morning and late evening as many Malaysians like to buy fresh ingredients for cooking. *Pasar malam* or night-markets are also popular.

Bargaining is generally only acceptable in the markets and at the roadside stalls. As a rule, prices for goods sold in street markets and small stores are negotiable but the prices are fixed in large department stores. Some smaller shops may give small discounts if asked, particularly if a large amount is purchased. If you are unsure, make a polite request to determine the response. Prices at the Kinabalu park are generally fixed.

**Accommodation**

For a proper appreciation of Kinabalu it is essential to spend at least a couple of nights in the park, preferably more. A variety of accommodation is available at Park HQ, Poring and Mesilau as well as at Panar Laban (at 3,272 metres/10,735 feet on the Summit Trail of Mount Kinabalu).

You can choose from a range of chalets, cabins, and lodges sleeping anything from 2 to 10 people, or for economy stay in the hostels. Camping is only an option at Poring, Serinsim and Sayap. For the latter two, visitors should bring their own tents since these cannot be hired in the park except at Poring.

There are two restaurants at Park HQ, and one each at Poring, Mesilau and Panar Laban. At Poring food is also available at roadside stalls just outside the park.

For those who prefer to do it

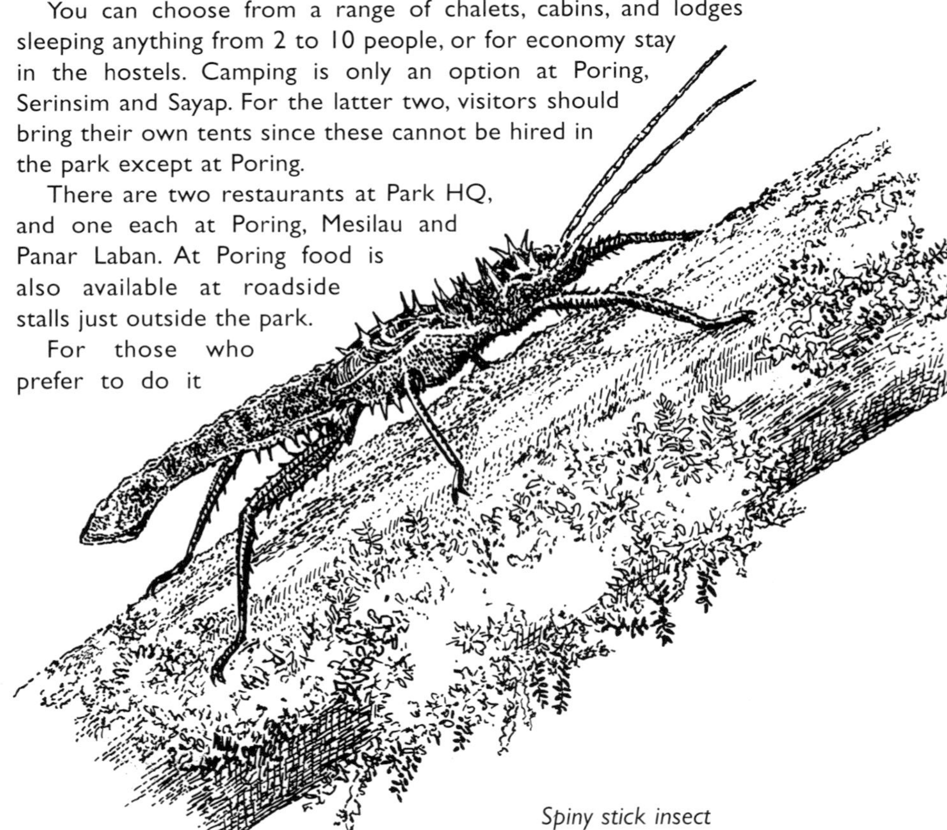

*Spiny stick insect*

themselves, self-catering is also possible in the park. However, you should buy most of your food before departure as there is more variety in KK. Basic supplies are also available at Kundasang and Ranau (for Mesilau and Poring) at Kota Belud (for Sayap) and at Kota Marudu (for Serinsim).

With the increasing popularity and accessibility of the park, accommodation can become booked up well in advance at certain times of year, so it is important to book well ahead of time. All the accommodation in the park is booked through Kinabalu Nature Resort in KK and must be paid for in advance.

**Kinabalu Park HeadQuarters**

| *Type* | *No. of Persons* |
|---|---|
| Hostel | 98 persons |
| Chalets: | |
| Rajah Lodge | 10 persons |
| Kinabalu Lodge | 8 persons |
| Nepenthes Villa (8 units) | 4 persons/unit |
| Double Storey Cabin | 7 persons |
| Single Storey Cabin | 5 persons |
| Duplex Cabin (4 Units) | 6 persons/unit |
| Annex Suite (4 units) | 4 persons/unit |
| Twin Bed Cabin (10 units) | 2 persons/unit |

Self-catering facilities in some chalets. No camping. Restaurants – The Mt. Kinabalu & The Kinabalu Balsam

**Poring Hot Springs**

| *Type* | *No. of Persons* |
|---|---|
| Hostel | 68 persons |
| Chalets: | |
| Poring Rajawali 1 Chalet | 6 persons |
| Poring Rajawali 2 Chalet | 6 persons |
| Poring Cabin A (Old) | 6 persons |
| Poring Cabin B (New) | 4 persons |

Self-catering facilities in all chalets. Camping is available. You may use your own tents or hire them from the Kinabalu Nature Resort office at Poring. Restaurant – Kalibambang, across the Mamut River; local food stalls just outside the entrance.

**Mesilau**

| *Type* | *No. of Persons* |
|---|---|
| Bishop's Head 1 & 2 Hostel | 96 persons |

## Minimal Impact Code

• Kinabalu has many rare and endangered plants and animals. It is important that you do not harm, disturb or remove any of them.

• Do not encourage trade in living plants or animals, or items produced from threatened natural resources.

• When walking, stay on identifiable paths and follow your guide.

• When near animals, avoid making undue noise or movement, or doing anything to disturb them. Use binoculars rather than trying to get too close.

By assisting in these small ways, you will help to promote responsible tourism for the future. Remember, you are one of the fortunate few to visit this place. Don't spoil the experience for others.

***Take nothing but photographs and fond memories, leave nothing but footprints and smiling faces.***

| Chalets: | |
|---|---|
| Low's Peak | 6 persons |
| St. John's Peak | 6 persons |
| Ugly Sisters Peak | 4 persons |
| Donkey's Ears Peak 1 | 4 persons |
| Donkey's Ears Peak 2 | 4 persons |
| King Edward Peak | 4 persons |
| Witti Range (4 units) | 6 persons/unit |
| Crocker Range (12 units) | 6 persons/unit |

Self-catering facilities in chalets and hostels. No camping. Restaurant – The Mesilau.

**Panar Laban**

| *Type* | *No. of Persons* |
|---|---|
| Laban Rata Resthouse | 54 persons (in 2-4 person rooms) |
| Gunting Lagadan Hut | 44 persons |
| Waras Hut | 12 persons |
| Panar Laban Hut | 12 persons |
| Sayat-Sayat Hut | 12 persons |

Self-catering in all huts except Laban Rata resthouse. No camping. Heaters and one blanket supplied for those staying at Laban Rata. Extra blankets are charged extra. The other huts have much more basic facilities – only a thin mattress, but sleeping bags and blankets can be hired on request through Kinabalu Nature Resort at park HQ. Restaurant – The Laban Rata.

*Bird's nest fern*

**PROTECTING THE PARK**

The park is a protected place, and everyone visiting Kinabalu and other natural places in Malaysia has an important role to play in ensuring it stays this way for present and future visitors. All wildlife is protected in the park and even the smallest change can have a big impact upon plant and animal communities that have evolved in isolation for centuries. Park rules and guidelines are clearly displayed in the park. Most of them are common sense to most people, but it does no harm to be reminded.

The following simple rules and guidelines makes a big difference in preserving natural areas like Kinabalu.

1. Do not destroy or remove any plant or animal. It is an offence to remove plants, animals and to shoot, trap and/or collect animals.

2. Leave the park cleaner than you found it. Dispose of rubbish appropriately and clean up if need be after those who don't.

3. Pets are not allowed into the park as they may introduce diseases to isolated populations or may escape and go wild.
4. Leave radios and cassette players at home as the music not only disturbs the wildlife but also those who want to see it. Be considerate of other visitors who may be engaged in activities like birdwatching that require silence.
5. Avoid buying and taking excessively packaged products into the park as the waste has to be disposed of somewhere. Take as little as possible on walks and return all rubbish to Park HQ and place in a bin (recycling bin where possible).

**Visitors Can Play A Role in Kinabalu**

The joint objectives of conservation and rural development in Kinabalu require the commitment of both visitors and participants in the tourism industry. All parties can take on a more active role to minimise negative impacts and adopt more sustainable practices. Tourists can contribute by making discerning choices before and during their trips and by providing feedback afterwards. In addition, ensuring that local people benefit from tourism creates an incentive for them to preserve natural habitats. Environmentally responsible nature tourism involves:

- travel to undisturbed areas to appreciate their natural and cultural features.
- minimal visitor impact on the natural surroundings.
- only development that does not exhaust or degrade the resource upon which it depends.
- promoting and supporting conservation efforts in the host area.
- providing opportunities for the beneficial involvement of local communities.

Kinabalu has a range of action and adventure to suit everybody's tastes, from serious sports enthusiasts to armchair adventurers.

# Activities and Adventure

The most popular activity is climbing the famous Summit Trail, but many other activities are also available. The summit climb takes a minimum of two days, but if you have time, a week allows more leisure to explore the mountain fully, allowing you to visit both Poring and Mesilau, as well as time to walk the forest trails around Park HQ and to enjoy the cool air. Many visitors take advantage of the hot sulphur pools at Poring after the strenuous climb to relax and renew tired muscles. Other activities such as mountain-biking are becoming more popular and various routes can be explored around the park boundaries, although the park does not supply bikes. For runners, the annual international climbathon is another increasingly popular challenge. Above all, the park's natural riches enjoy an international reputation among plant enthusiasts and birdwatchers.

# Visitor Activities

### Trekking

Trekking within the Park is generally restricted to shorter trails taking no more than a day. The majority of trails take less than half a day. These generally require no special abilities, but it is wise to check with the Park authorities in advance in case longer trails are blocked by landslides or broken bridges. Good footwear is essential, especially in wet weather.

### Climbing

Climbing Kinabalu (Low's Peak) is within the reach of most visitors as long as they are reasonably fit and well prepared. Kinabalu's other peaks are not for the average visitor and should only be climbed by those with experience, or at least by those who have experienced climbers in their group. The climb to the eastern plateau, while not requiring specialist knowledge, can be quite challenging and demands a good head for heights. The Park requires all climbers to be accompanied by Park guides. This is particularly important if you are using trails other than the standard climb to Low's Peak, but even for this a guide is compulsory.

### Camping

Camping is encouraged only at Poring Hot Springs. Tents, pillows and blankets can be hired at Poring, or you can bring your own. Food is available at the restaurant on the other side of the Mamut river or from the stalls just outside the park entrance. It is also possible to camp at both the Sayap and Serinsim stations, but you will need a 4-wheel drive to reach them and must bring all your own gear, including food, as there are no visitor facilities at either place. Camping is not permitted elsewhere in the Park.

### Wildlife watching

Larger animals are rare and difficult to see but a lot of interest and pleasure can be had watching smaller creatures, particularly insects. Butterflies, moths and beetles are particularly diverse and colourful and can be examined closely clustered on walls or bushes under lamps in the early morning.

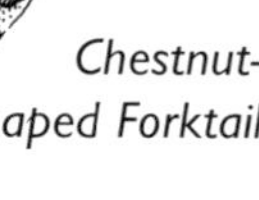

*Chestnut-naped Forktail*

### Birdwatching

Both Kinabalu Park HQ and Mesilau Nature Resort are excellent places for watching montane birds, especially in the early mornings when many birds are hawking insects around the lamp posts. Poring Hot springs is good for lowland species, such as spiderhunters and sunbirds. Over 300 species have been recorded from the park.

### Plant spotting

Kinabalu is one of the richest centres of plant diversity in the world and is an excellent place to observe a wide range of plants. Orchids, rhododendrons and pitcher-plants are particularly showy. The pitcher-plants *Nepenthes villosa* and *Nepenthes rajah* are not found anywhere else in the world and both are easily visible on Kinabalu. Likewise, many orchids are found only on the mountain. The mountain garden at the Park HQ and the Orchid Conservation Centre at Poring are excellent places for more detailed observation of Kinabalu's plants, where many rare species are easily seen. Kinabalu is one of the few places in Borneo where the giant-flowered Rafflesia is easily accessible, though whether or not it will be flowering is largely a matter of luck. The Sabah Parks staff at Poring should know whether any are blooming at the time of your visit.

### Photography

The Kinabalu Park provides endless opportunities for the photographer – from the changing views of the mountain to the thousands of plants and animals that live there. You will almost certainly need more film than you think. White or pale flowers are particularly difficult to take with flash and a useful item is a light reflector to reflect the sunlight onto the object you are photographing. (For further advice on film, and what equipment to take, see **Equipment**, page 21.)

### Scientific projects

The Kinabalu Park has an active core of research staff carrying out a variety of projects. One of the major ongoing projects is a collaboration between the Sabah Parks and the Royal Botanic Gardens of Kew, England, to document the mountain's botanical diversity. Three volumes have already been published from this huge task – Ferns and their allies; Orchids, and Gymnosperms and Non-orchid Monocots. Volume 4, covering the remainder, will be by far the largest. All scientific research carried out by foreigners requires a government permit and those interested in working in the Park should contact the Deputy Director (Research), Sabah Parks, Kota Kinabalu, well in advance.

### Climbathon

For the last 13 years the Mount Kinabalu International Climbathon has been an annual event in September/October. This is literally a race to the summit and back. The record so far is a mere 2 hours and 42 minutes. Most people take 4-5 hours to reach Panar Laban, let alone the summit and back! The race first started as a competition among the Park staff aimed at improving rescue efforts on the mountain in the development of a Rapid Reaction Rescue Squad and, as such, was first held in 1984. It was not until 1987 that outsiders were allowed to take part. Following the success of the 1987 national race, the Climbathon went international in 1988, earning itself the title of the "toughest mountain race in the world". Indeed the Climbathon is not for the faint-hearted. Its gruelling 21km (13 mile) route over a more than 2,250m (7,357 feet) ascent, and the punishing pace, test even the most experienced (participants who don't finish within 4 hours are automatically disqualified), but every year more mountain runners take part, including the world's best.

In the early days, Nepalese Gurkha runners dominated the men's race, with Sundar Kumar Linthap winning from 1988 to 1990, followed by Kusang Gurung from 1991-1993. In 1994 the crown was taken over by local Guianus Salagan, before he was overtaken in turn by Ian Holmes of Great Britain in 1997. Holmes still holds the title and the record of 2 hours 42 minutes and 7 seconds for the fastest race.

The achievements of the Salagan family include not only those of Guianus, but also those of his older sister Hasny, who has won the women's race a remarkable total of 5 times, more than any other. Her last three wins from 1994 to 1996 mirror those of her brother, who won the men's race in the same years, and she still holds the women's record of 3 hours, 18 minutes and 36 seconds for the summit race.

In 1997 the women's race was shortened and for that year, 1998 and 1999, the ladies raced only to Panar Laban (3262m/10,703feet) and back. Another local girl, Danny Gongot, held the women's record of 2 hours 3 minutes and 47 seconds for this shorter distance, until the 1999 race which was won by Scottish chemist Angela Mudge, setting a new record of 1 hour, 58 minutes, 23 seconds. But Hasny still remains unchallenged queen of the 21 km summit race and in 2000 the ladies will once again race the same route as the men.

**Mountain Running**

On the back of international recognition of the Climbathon as one of the world's hardest mountain races, the 15th World Mountain Running Trophy race was held in the Kinabalu Park in September 1999 under the auspices of the International Amateur Athletics Federation. It was the first time this race had been held outside Europe and it attracted more than 300 world class athletes. Not as steep as the Climbathon route, the race covered 12.5km (8.5 miles) of forest trails around Park HQ and the new Pandanus trail was specially built to fulfil requirements for the race.

**Mountain Biking**

Mountain-bike racing is also becoming popular in Sabah and the International Mount Kinabalu Mountain Bike Race, another annual event, was started in 1998. This is a tough 27 kilometre (17 mile) race through the villages of Kaung and Kiau on the southern slopes of the mountain where Low, Whitehead and others passed on their historic ascents.

The record for the men's Mountain Bike Race (1 hour 42 minutes) is held by Guianus Salagan, better known for his achievements in the Climbathon. His victory in the 1999 Mountain Bike race confirmed the extreme physical challenge of the course which has a 4 kilometre, 600 metre (2 mile, 2,000 foot) climb just before the finish.

Another mountain-biking event, circling the Kinabalu massif in four days, is also likely to become an annual event. After the first circumnavigation of the mountain in 1999, a long distance mountain-bike race following the same route is planned to enter the Sabah sports calendar in the year 2000. For those not interested in racing but wishing to try this impressive circumnavigation, the route can be completed in 4 days of moderately hard riding with an average of 7-9 hours riding a day. The route description can be obtained from the Sabah Sports and Recreation Society (see **Address Book**, p121–122).

## Things to do

- Watch the sun rise from the top of South-east Asia's highest mountain.
- Relax in hot sulphur-water pools.
- Trek through mountain forests.
- Spot some of Borneo's rarest birds and elusive mammals.
- Discover an abundance of plant life, including orchids, rafflesia and the world's largest pitcher plants.
- Camp out in tropical rainforest.
- Enter the Climbathon, the world's toughest mountain race.
- Circumnavigate the mountain on a mountain bike.
- Play golf beneath the towering mountain pinnacles (just outside the park).
- Visit the war memorial and learn about the mountain's historic past.

### Hang-gliding

Hang-gliding may become a sport of the future on Mount Kinabalu, but at present it is not possible without a lot of pre-organisation and government approval which can take time to secure. In addition, all equipment has to be brought in from overseas. A few days before the 1999 Mountain Running race, however, the inaugural Hang-gliding Kinabalu Challenge was held at the Kinabalu Golf Course, attended by hang-gliding experts from around the world. Participants in the inaugural challenge described the setting as one of the most exciting and magnificent they had experienced, as well as one of the most difficult, and it is hoped to hold the World Hang-gliding Championships here in 2003 and see what possibilities for the future the sport holds.

Further information on these events, and specialist tour operators, are available from the Sabah Tourism Promotion Corporation office in Kota Kinabalu. (see **Address Book**, p121–122)

### Golf

In addition to enjoying the attractions of the natural environment, a visit to Kinabalu also has something for the golf enthusiast. The 18-hole Kinabalu Golf Course on the Pinosok Plateau above Kundasang is Malaysia's highest and must be one of the world's most spectacular, set as it is beneath the majestic peaks and pinnacles of the mountain. For the serious enthusiast, the Mesilau resort, almost backing the Golf Course is the best place to stay. Transport can be arranged through the resort, and golf clubs can be hired from the Golf Club (tel: 889-448).

**War Memorial**

When Sabah (then North Borneo) was liberated from the Japanese after World War Two, a memorial was set up at Kundasang in memory of those who had lost their lives. In particular, the memorial commemorates the allied soldiers who died on the infamous Death March, just before the war ended. 2,400 Australian and British prisoners-of-war were forced to walk the 240kms (150 miles) from the town of Sandakan on Sabah's east coast to Ranau, in horrendous conditions on only 70 grams (2½ ounces) of rice a day. Only 6 survived, aided by a local Dusun farmer who risked his own life to save them. In fact the memorial was erected not so much as a reminder of the horrors of war but as a "dedication to the brotherhood of man as exemplified by the trust and respect the people of Borneo, Australia and Britain had for each other during those dark days", in the words of the architect.

## ORGANISED ACTIVITIES

**Park HQ.**

| | |
|---|---|
| Mountain garden | at 0900,1200,1500 |
| Guided Walk | at 1100 |
| Slide show | at 1400 (and 1930 at weekends) |

A fee of only a few ringgit is charged for each activity
You can buy a "package" ticket for all 3.

**Poring**

| | |
|---|---|
| Canopy Walkway | 0900 to 1600, guided walk at 0800 |
| Butterfly Farm | 0900 to 1600, guided walk at 1100 (not Monday) |
| Tropical Garden | at 1330 |
| Orchid Conservation Centre | at 1430 |
| Night Walk | By arrangement |

A fee of only a few ringgit is charged for each activity
"Package" tickets are also available

**Mesilau**

Guided Nature Walk

| | |
|---|---|
| Monday to Friday | 0930, 1100, 1400 |
| Saturday and Sunday | 0730, 1030, 1400 |

# Life on the Mountain

Kinabalu is one of the world's 'hotspots' of biodiversity, and one of its main attractions for many visitors, from early explorers to today's climbers, is the rich array of plant and animal life that can be seen.

Early scientific interest in the mountain was fuelled by the many spectacular and often strange plants found by early collectors, including such superlatives as the Rajah Brooke's Pitcher Plant. Many of these early explorers were associated with the horticultural nurseries in Europe, at a time when collecting exotic hothouse plants, especially orchids, was becoming increasingly popular amongst the rich.

Today many visitors are also drawn by the abundant birdlife, the impressive range of insects – many endemic to the mountain – or the chance of coming across one of the more elusive mammals. Whether it is plants, animals, or simply the sheer wonder of the landscape, the park offers a rich and rewarding experience for anyone with an interest in the natural world.

## ENDEMISM AND DIVERSITY

Kinabalu has long been known for its biological diversity and high levels of endemism, ie, species which occur only on the mountain or within the Kinabalu Park and are found nowhere else in the world. For example, Kinabalu possesses one of the world's richest orchid floras with more than half (746) of the estimated 1,400 species for Borneo. Another frequently quoted figure is that for the ferns. There are over 600 species on Kinabalu (more than in the whole African continent, which has about 500 species), 50 of which are found nowhere else.

Today Kinabalu is studied more than other mountain in Borneo, so some species that are presently thought to be endemic to the mountain may yet be found elsewhere as other Borneo mountains are explored further. However, none come anywhere near Kinabalu in height (Borneo's second highest mountain, neighbouring Tamboyukon, reaches only 2579 metres [8,461 feet]) and it seems that this magnificent mountain really is one of the world's most important biological sites.

Why should the mountain have developed such an incredible array of plant life? The answers lie in its distant past as well as in its more recent evolution. First and foremost, Kinabalu is situated in the one of the richest plant regions of the world, covering a wide climatic range from near sea level to freezing ground conditions below the summit. The jagged terrain and the diversity of rocks and soils have combined with the instability caused by periods of glaciation, and other catastrophic events such El Nino droughts, to produce ideal conditions for evolution and speciation to take place. Evolution is driven by change. Because they are immobile, plants cannot escape changing conditions as easily as animals so they must adapt or die, and in adapting have evolved many endemic species.

This diversity is greatest in the lowland forests, but most of Kinabalu's endemics are found in the mountain forests, particularly on ultramafic soils. Kinabalu is the richest place in the world for the tropical pitcher plants *Nepenthes*. Ten out of the approximately 36 species in Borneo are found on this single mountain, where they reach an unparalleled level of spectacular elegance. Five, restricted to the ultramafic soils, are found nowhere else.

Periods of small scale extinction have also occurred in cases where plants have been limited to restricted areas, particularly after castastrophic events. Some studies have recorded about 22% local extinction within the ferns on Kinabalu within 10 years and observations after

### Malesia

The latest botanical surveys of the mountain estimate a staggering 5,000 to 6,000 species (excluding mosses and liverworts but including ferns) on Kinabalu, a figure that becomes even more amazing when you consider that this comprises more than 10% of all the plants recorded from the biogeographical region known as Malesia.

Malesia (pronounced "Ma-lee-sia") is a huge area containing the Malay Peninsula, Sumatra, Java, Borneo, the Philippines, Sulawesi and New Guinea. It should not be confused with the geopolitical entity known as Malaysia, though Malaysia is totally encompassed within the Malesian region.

THE MANY WATERFALLS ENCOUNTERED ON THE MOUNTAIN TRAILS ARE ICY-COLD AND MOST SPECTACULAR DURING AND AFTER THE MONSOON RAINS.

ABOVE: AT PORING, A WALKWAY ALLOWS THE VISITOR TO ENTER THE HIDDEN WORLD OF THE LOWLAND FOREST CANOPY.

LEFT: MOUNTAIN BIKES HAVE BECOME AN INCREASINGLY POPULAR WAY TO EXPLORE THE LOWER SLOPES OF THE MOUNTAIN.

OPPOSITE ABOVE: FIXED ROPES HELP TREKKERS TO NEGOTIATE THE STEEPER PARTS OF THE SUMMIT TRAIL.

OPPOSITE BELOW: AT PORING HOT SPRINGS VISITORS CAN RELAX IN A WARM, NATURAL SULPHUR BATH.

ABOVE TOP: THE ANNUAL CLIMBATHON ATTRACTS INTERNATIONAL COMPETITION.

ABOVE: AN ACTIVE CORE OF RESEARCH STAFF IS ENGAGED IN A VARIETY OF PROJECTS.

LEFT: WOODEN STEPS ASSIST THE VISITOR ON THE STEEPER PARTS OF THE SUMMIT TRAIL.

the most recent 1998 El Nino drought suggest that as many as 50% of the epiphytes were killed off on certain parts of the mountain. On the other hand many animals can move away from adverse conditions and endemism is much less, at least among the larger animals. Nevertheless some groups, particularly among the insects, have developed a remarkable degree of diversity. Take the butterflies as an example. Of the more than 900 butterflies known from Borneo, over 600 (two-thirds) are found in the Kinabalu Park, making it a hotspot of butterfly diversity not only in Borneo but in the whole of South-east Asia. Butterflies are mainly creatures of the lowlands, however, and while diversity is high, endemism is low.

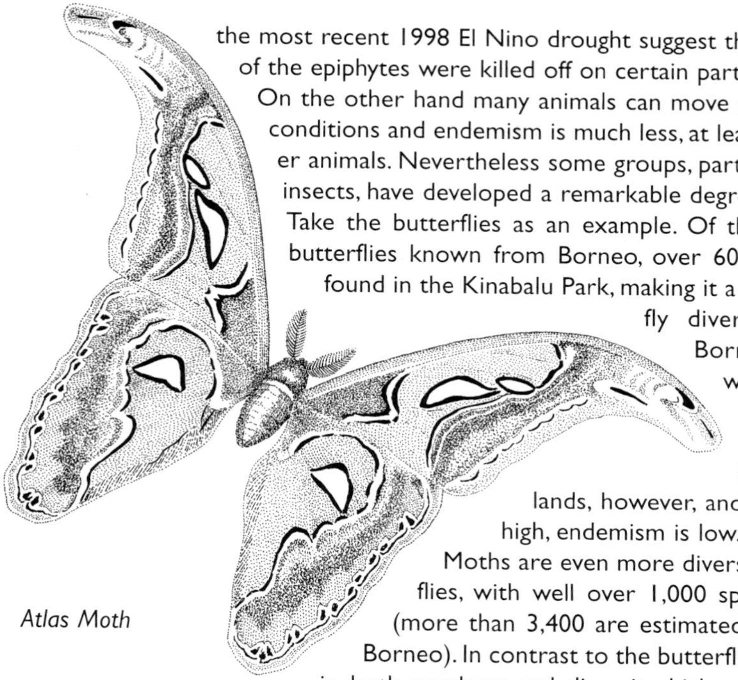

*Atlas Moth*

Moths are even more diverse than the butterflies, with well over 1,000 species on Kinabalu (more than 3,400 are estimated for the whole of Borneo). In contrast to the butterflies, moths increase in both numbers and diversity higher up the mountain, and many species are endemic. Around 2,000 metres (6,500 feet) on Kinabalu, endemism reaches about 50%. Above this height, the level of diversity drops and only four species are recorded above 3,000 metres (10,000 feet).

Mammals and birds which can move easily over large areas and are most common in lowland habitats are less likely to develop endemism. Though several bird species were once thought to be endemic to Kinabalu, it is now known that they all also occur on Sabah's other two highest mountains, Tamboyukon (2,579 metres/8,461 feet) which lies 20 kilometres (12 miles) to the north, but still within Kinabalu Park, and Trus Madi (2,642 metres/8,668 feet), 50 kilometres (30 miles) to the east, well outside the park boundary.

Of the mammals, only two, the Black Shrew (*Suncus ater*) and the Kinabalu Shrew (*Crocidura baluensis*) are endemic to the mountain. However, the Black Shrew is known from only a single specimen, collected at 1,700 metres (5,600 feet), and the Kinabalu Shrew was, until very recently, regarded only as a form of the very widespread South-east Asian White-toothed Shrew (*Crocidura fuliginosa*). The opposite situation prevails regarding the Kinabalu Ferret-badger (*Melogale personata everetti*) which was thought to be endemic to Kinabalu and nearby Gunung Tamboyukon. This animal is now recognised as only a sub-species of the ferret-badger that occurs widely across South-east Asia. The situation could change, however, depending on whose taxonomic views hold sway at the time. Similarly, the well-known Kinabalu Rat that occurs around the mountain huts at Laban Rata and has been recorded as high as 3,100 metres (10,200 feet), was once thought to be endemic, but is now regarded only as a high altitude form of the common lowland Long-tailed Giant Rat (*Leopoldamys sabanus*).

## VEGETATION ZONES AND PLANT LIFE.

Vegetation zones on Kinabalu are largely determined by altitude, but within the main forest zones many variations have developed, affected by differences in the soil, slope, availability of water and degree of exposure, eg, a sheltered valley will have taller, more luxuriant vegetation compared to an exposed ridge at the same altitude.

### Lowland dipterocarp forest.

Lowland dipterocarp forest occurs mainly to the north and east, covering about 35% of the Park. The forest canopy can reach as high as 50 metres (160 feet). It is dark and dim and there is little ground cover. Trees in the family Dipterocarpaceae are dominant.

These lowland dipterocarp forests support the highest concentrations of animal life because the stature of the trees provides a much greater variety of habitats and food. Dipterocarps themselves are not a main source of food. They fruit rarely but when they do, they fruit "*en masse*". At these times, whole hillsides are covered in drifts of cream, yellow or pink from flowers or young fruits, making you realise just how dominant the dipterocarps are in what little remains of Borneo's undisturbed lowland forests.

The lowland forests are also rich in a variety of fruit trees such as durian, rambutan and Tarap, as well as figs. Figs have been proven to be one of the most important sources of food, especially for monkeys and civets and for larger birds such as hornbills, barbets and pigeons. For birdwatchers it is always worthwhile spending some time beneath a large fruiting fig, since large mixed species feeding parties are often attracted to its abundant fruits. While other fruits can be very seasonal, there is always a fig fruiting somewhere.

### Ultramafic soils

The underlying rock also has a strong influence on vegetation zones. In areas where ultramafic rocks occur, the vegetation changes abruptly. Ultramafic forests cover about 16% of the park. Here the soils are low in phosphates and high in iron, silica and metals poisonous to many plants. The high toxic content of these soils prevents many species from growing in these areas, so distinct communities containing rare and unusual species and many endemics have developed. The pitcher plants *Nepenthes villosa* and *N.rajah* and the slipper orchids, *Paphiopedilum rothschildianum* and *P.dayanum* are found only on ultramafic soils in the Kinabalu park.

### Lower montane oak–chestnut forest.

Above about 1,200 metres (4,000 feet) the lowland trees peter out as conifers and oaks become more dominant. The trees are smaller, the canopy reaching 25 to 30 metres (80 to 100 feet) at most. Because of the cooler climate, peat begins to develop and mosses become common. More light reaches the ground so there is both a thicker ground cover and thicker development of epiphytes, especially orchids. Other trees that are particularly common in this montane forest are members of the eucalyptus and tea families as well as conifers such as *Dacrydium*, *Podocarpus*, *Dacrycarpus*, *Agathis* and *Phyllocladus* which have no flowers.

Co-dominant with the conifers are the oaks. Borneo is at the hub of the Malesian oak kingdom, with over 100 species in the oak family Fagaceae recorded on the island. Twelve chestnuts and almost 50 oaks occur on Kinabalu, their fruit ranging from shiny little pixie caps sitting in a dainty cup, to stony kernels almost covered by the thick, massive coat, except for a hole at the top, as big as a child's fist. Fallen acorns and spiny chestnut cases are common along the trails.

Oaks and chestnuts are also an important source of food, not only for animals such as squirrels who can gnaw through even the hardest kernel, but also for wild pigs. In the past, when large tracts of forest still covered Borneo, pigs formed large herds migrating up to the oak–chestnut forest in the fruiting season. Here they could also build 'nests' in which to give birth, taking advantage of the abundant food.

**Upper montane forest.**

Above about 2,200 metres (7,200 feet), where swirling mists blanket the forest for much of the day, lies the moss or cloud forest. Here the trees are thickly cloaked and shawled with mosses and liverworts dripping with moisture. Orchids are abundant, both in the ground cover and as epiphytes, and members of the rhododendron family, as well as conifers, become particularly common at these altitudes. It was in these forests that Sir Hugh Low found one of his most spectacular plants – the magnificent Low's Rhododendron, its huge golden heads almost glowing in the misty forest. The rhododendrons are some of Kinabalu's loveliest flowers and while Kinabalu cannot lay claim to the vast numbers of rhododendrons as grow in the forests of China and Nepal, 24 out of the 50 described for Borneo grow on the mountain and five are found nowhere else.

**Sub-alpine zone.**

By about 3,300 metres (11,000 feet), a sub-alpine zone has developed. The trees are gnarled and stunted, forming a shrub community with conifers and rhododendrons dominant. The scarlet, thimble-sized flowers of the Heath Rhododendron (*R.ericoides*) grow in thickets here together with the larger red-flowered Box-leaved Rhododendron (*R.buxifolium*) which can be spectacular when in full bloom around March and April. In open soggy patches, grassy meadow-like associations develop, consisting of buttercups, potentillas, eyebright and gentians, more familiar from temperate meadows. Shrub raspberries are common – a favourite food of the Mountain Blackbird. In cracks and crevices in the rocks, tough little mountain orchids find a root-hold, looking like drifts of snow when in full bloom. The tree-line here is determined not by altitude but by soil, or rather, by the lack of it. The fierce winds and torrential rains make it impossible for most plants to survive higher than about 3,700 metres (12,000 feet). In sheltered places and in rock crevices, a few dwarf, twisted bonsai-like shrubs struggle for life while sparse tough grasses barely survive in sheltered shallow hollows filled with sand scoured from the surrounding granite rocks.

## ANIMAL LIFE

### Butterflies and Moths

Some of the most abundant and conspicuous creatures are the butterflies and moths. Butterflies are nearly all day fliers and are most common in the lowlands. One of the best places to see them is at Poring Hot Springs.

Moths, on the other hand, are mainly night fliers and are more common at higher elevations. At Park HQ they are attracted in abundance to lights at the chalets and around the street lamps, particularly after rain.

The great majority of these moths are so tiny that most people would not give them a second glance. Some of the larger moths, however, are quite spectacular. One such is the huge reddish-brown Atlas Moth (*Attacus atlas*) with its rich hues and translucent wing patches. With a wing-span of 25 centimetres (10 inches), the Atlas Moth is recognised as the largest moth in the world. The Moon Moth (*Argema maenas*) is more rarely seen but is perhaps even more beautiful, its pale powdery-green hindwings extended into long drawn-out tails. A commoner species at both lowland and montane altitudes is the duller Zebra Moth (*Lyssa mentoetius)* with its muted grey and white colours.

Amongst the easiest moths to recognise as a group are the hawk moths, readily distinguished by their long narrow forewings and triangular shape when at rest. Many are important pollinators of scented night-flowering plants, and one species is recorded as entering bee hives to steal the honey

Some hawk moths may emerge from their chrysalises gregariously under certain weather conditions and on a few occasions, when monsoon storms have broken after a long, dry period, the bushes along the roadside at Park HQ have literally been covered with hawkmoths, providing a veritable feast for the early morning birds at the streetlamps. In recent years however, the number of moths attracted to the lights appears to be decreasing, perhaps because many more hotels and chalets are springing up around the park, so the insects are not so concentrated.

### Beetles

Beetles are the largest group of insects in the world with over 350,000 species recognised worldwide, but over 95% of them are less than a centimetre (half an inch) in

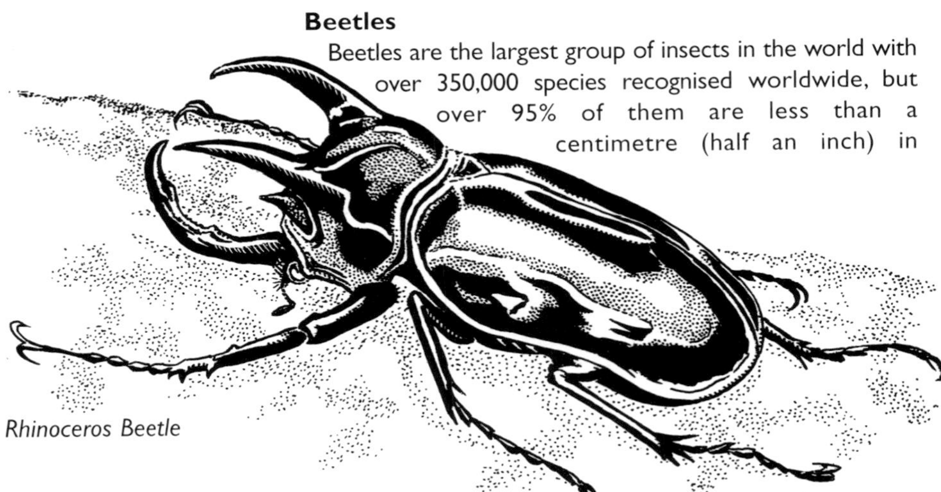

*Rhinoceros Beetle*

length. No one knows how many species of beetles live on Kinabalu but they show an amazing diversity of shape, size, colour and life-style.

Some of the most conspicuous are the shiny black rhinoceros beetles that sport long black horns on their heads and the brown and black stag beetles with greatly enlarged and strengthened jaws. Only the males bear these appendages which are used in trials of strength. The females of both groups, being smaller and lacking the fearsome ornamentation of the males look quite different. During the mating season, from September to October, these beetles are commonly attracted to lights at Park HQ, around Poring Hot Springs, and also at Mesilau.

One of the most attractive groups is the Chrysomelid or jewel beetles, often with a golden or green metallic sheen. These are day flying and feed on nectar in flowering trees, in which they are often found in large numbers. One recent study of canopy insects at Poring showed that Chrysomelid beetles made up almost one quarter of the total beetle inhabitants, and recent studies in Sarawak have shown that Chrysomelid beetles are of considerable importance in the pollination of dipterocarps and probably of other flowering trees.

Most curious of all, though, must be the Trilobite beetles of the genus *Duliticola*. It is the female of the species that is the most striking, retaining its almost prehistoric larval form even when sexually mature. At Park HQ, an undescribed species, black with a striking orange rim, can often be seen crawling slowly over the rotting logs on which it feeds along the trails. Another, smaller, darker species that lacks the striking orange rim, *Duliticola paradoxa*, has been recorded from Poring.

### Longhorn beetles

One of the biggest groups of beetles in the Park are the longhorns, easily distinguished by their long antennae. The species are either day or night fliers, most showy ones flying by day, feeding mainly on flowers. These beetles have particularly strong jaws, which are used by the females to bite holes in living trees in which to lay their eggs. When the larvae hatch they bore tunnels through the wood as they feed. The larval stage can last for several years and many species are considered to be timber pests. Other beetles may feed on fungi or decaying wood, animal dung or fresh young leaves, or even on other beetles.

**Stick and Leaf Insects.**

About 100 out of the 300 or so Borneo species of the curiously camouflaged stick insects are recorded from Kinabalu, including the longest insect in the world, *Phoebaeticus serratipes*. A specimen of this species, collected in Singapore, measured 55.5 centimetres (21 inches) from the tip of the fore-legs to the tip of the hind-legs, though most average about 30 centimetres (12 inches). Another species, the spiny *Haaniela echinata* found in the lowland forests around Poring, lays the largest known eggs in the insect world, almost a centimetre (half an inch) in length, which take up to a year to hatch.

Stick insects are masters of mimicry and are superbly camouflaged, sometimes ornamented with tough spines, small rough projections or paler spots that look like patches of moss. When disturbed their main defence is to remain absolutely stiff and still, like the sticks they so closely resemble. They are most active at night, feeding on leaves in the forest.

Closely related are the beautiful leaf insects, which are just as well camouflaged, even to patches of "insect damage" along the edge of their "leaf" wings. Leaf insects were regarded by the ancient Chinese as magical "leaves" that could walk away from trees when felled; even other insects are fooled by them, to the extent that leaf-insects in captivity with other herbivores, may end up being chewed themselves.

**Migrating herdsmen**

Migrating herdsmen ant associations are found only in South-east Asia, and were recently discovered to be common in Kinabalu Park. Large groups of these ants 'herd' their small reddish-brown mealy-bug 'cattle' on the young parts of plants that produce the nutrient-rich sap on which the mealy-bugs feed. The ants gather so closely over their 'cattle', protecting them from rain and sun, that it is impossible to see the bugs beneath. They 'milk' them by stroking them with their antennae to stimulate the release of sweet honey-dew droplets – food for the ants. When the plants are older, and producing less sap, the 'herder' ants migrate, carrying their 'cattle' to fresh pastures.

### Ants

The commonest insects in the Kinabalu Park, at least in terms of mass, are probably the ants, which are most abundant in the lowland forest. Ants formed more than 50% of the total individuals collected in a canopy-fogging experiment at Poring Hot Springs in 1998, and they have developed a staggering array of life-styles, including many mutually beneficial associations with plants. Several of these relationships can be observed in the Kinabalu Park.

Species of the small secondary forest trees *Macaranga,* are often associated with ants. Usually the ants make their nests in the hollow stems and rush to the plant's defence if it is attacked by herbivores. Ants living in association with certain rattan palms build their nests in the old hollow leaf sheaths that the palm seems to retain particularly for this purpose, and protect the young shoots from predators in the same way. These ants also maintain extensive colonies of aphids on the same palm which provide them with food in the form of honey-dew. Certain ferns such as species of the epiphytic *Lecanopteris* have developed enlarged hollow rhizomes in which the ants build their nests, providing shelter in exchange for nutrients from the ants' waste products. Fallen pieces of the old, empty rhizomes are sometimes seen along the trails at Park HQ. Ants and other insects have also developed unusual relationships with the insect-eating pitcher plants. Though a few individuals may be drowned, dissolved and absorbed by the pitcher plant as food, the community as a whole benefits from the rich supply of nectar that the pitchers offer.

**BIRDS**

Together with insects, birds are the most visible animal inhabitants of the Park, though often they are more easily heard than seen. The most recent compilation of birds for Kinabalu, carried out by Sabah Parks staff in 1999, records 326 species, including migrants. These can be roughly divided into two loose groups – lowland birds rarely recorded above 1,000 metres (3,300 feet) and montane birds rarely recorded below 1,000 metres (3,300 feet) Obviously a considerable amount of overlap does occur and species such as the Mountain Serpent-eagle (*Spilornis kinabaluensis*) and the Wreathed Hornbill (*Aceros undulatus*) have been seen flying across the forested slopes as high as 3,300 metres (11,000 feet), though they are not resident at these elevations. The rather rare Mountain Serpent-eagle, distinguished from its more common cousin, the Crested Serpent-eagle (*Spilornis cheela*) by its darker plumage is confined to Borneo, where there are records from Gunung Murud and Gunung Mulu in northern Sarawak, in addition to Kinabalu.

Periods of severe drought on Kinabalu also affect the bird life, and in 1983 normally upper montane species such as the dark olive-green Mountain Blackeye (*Chlorocharis emiliae*) and red and black Mountain Blackbird (or Island Thrush) (*Turdus poliocephalus*) were frequently observed in small groups around Park HQ, though they are only rarely seen at this elevation at other times.

Diversity of birds on Kinabalu decreases with altitude, but this is made up for in numbers. Thus the Mountain Blackeye, though seen all the way up the Summit Trail above 2,000 metres (6,500 feet), is one of the two commonest birds around Panar Laban and made up 80% of the catch during mistnetting studies carried out by the Sabah Parks staff at the Paka Cave in 1999!. The other really common species up here is the Mountain Blackbird which has been recorded as nesting just below the summit. Found only on Mt. Kinabalu, Mt. Tamboyukon and Mt. Trus Madi in Borneo, the Mountain Blackbird also occurs in montane forests from the Philippines to Sumatra and New Guinea, in contrast to the Mountain Blackeye, not found outside Borneo, but present on most of the island's higher mountains.

Other species of the sub-alpine forests include the little brown Sunda Bush-warbler (*Cettia vulcania*), with its distinctive narrow buff eyebrow, that is also found in Java and Sumatra, and the tiny Short-tailed Bush-warbler or Bornean Stubtail (*Cettia whiteheadi*), distinguished by its white eyebrow and almost complete lack of any tail, which is confined to Borneo's higher mountains. Both these birds are most often seen above 2,000 metres (6,540 feet), where they tend to skulk about in undergrowth near the ground like small mice. The Blue or White-browed Shortwing (*Brachypteyx montana*), identified by its blue plumage with a white eyebrow and longer legs, prefers more open clearings and patches of bare rock near the tree-line. Widespread in South-east Asia, in Borneo it has so far been found only on both Trus Madi and Mulu in addition to Kinabalu. The female is reddish-brown below, while the male is dark blue all over.

Most notable of all the sub-alpine birds, however, is the Kinabalu Friendly Warbler (*Bradypterus accentor*), another skulker in the undergrowth. The bird has a streaked brown breast and is named for its confiding habit of hopping around between the feet of early climbers. Some years after the park was first established, one of the wardens noted sadly that the little birds were not seen so often as in the past and that the disturbance caused by a greater number of people walking the Summit Trail had probably driven them to quieter areas. Nevertheless, this bird can probably be said to be one of Kinabalu's most exclusive attractions – the only other records for it coming from Mt. Tamboyukon and the more distant Mt. Trus Madi, both far less accessible than Kinabalu.

## FISH, AMPHIBIANS AND REPTILES

Kinabalu's rivers and streams support about 40 species of freshwater fish, but virtually none are found above 1,500 metres (4,900 feet). The most common are the four species of the little *Gastromyzon* that graze on algae growing on boulders in the water and which are found up to just over 1,500 metres (4,900 feet). *Gastromyzon* are also called Sucker fish because of their ability to cling to rocks in fast moving waters by the adaptation of the lower fins into an efficient clasping sucker.

Sixty eight species of frogs are presently recorded from the Kinabalu Park, ranging from the lowlands right up to the Paka Cave at 3,050 metres (10,000 feet). Most of these can generally be regarded as lowland, however, and only four have been able to adapt to the harsh climatic conditions found at the Paka Cave and above.

One of these high-mountain frogs is the small blackish-brown *Philautus mjobergii*. This frog belongs to a group of moss forest specialists that have a most unusual lifestyle. The *Philautus* species in this group take advantage of the perpetual dampness in the cloud forest to lay their relatively large eggs in wet moss or under dead leaves; sometimes even in the decaying cups of the large pitcher plants. The eggs hatch into tiny froglets protected by the gelatinous egg case, never passing through a tadpole stage. The success of this strategy is shown by the fact that 30% of the frogs recorded from the montane forest are *Philautus* species. Most species however, need water for at least part of their life cycle and spend either all their lives near a stream or at least return to water to breed, whether it be a stream, rainwater accumulated in a hole in a tree or a temporary pool on the ground after a storm.

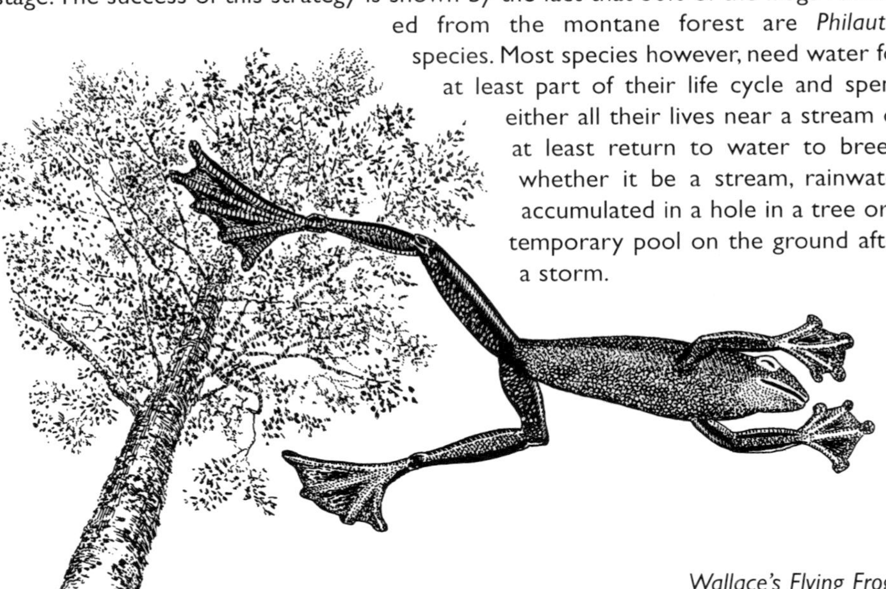

*Wallace's Flying Frog*

Borneo's most famous frog is Wallace's Flying Frog (*Rhacophorus nigropalmatus*). It has not been collected from the Park, but there are observation records from Poring. Wallace's Flying Frog, of course, does not fly, but it can glide quite long distances by spreading out the webbing between its fingers and its toes. Even its arms and legs are adorned with long flaps of skin to increase its surface area and thus slow its descent.

Though the other species in the tree frog family have their digits webbed to a greater or lesser degree, not all are recorded as being able to glide in the same way. All tree frogs, however, appear to have the striking ability to change their colour to some degree, which must help them blend in with the leaves on which they rest.

Snakes and lizards are relatively common in the lowlands, but they have not adapted as well as the frogs to the cool and wet conditions higher up, being cold-blooded and dependent on the warmth of the sun. Snakes in particular are not commonly seen because they try very hard to avoid detection. Lizards are a bit more visible. If staying at Poring, almost the first animals you encounter will probably be the little house geckos that follow wherever man makes a home; other geckos are forest dwellers. One species at Park HQ is also a glider.

## MAMMALS

Almost 100 of Borneo's mammals are recorded from Kinabalu but most live in the lowlands; very few are found above 1,700 metres (5,500 feet). Because hunting is still prevalent around the boundaries of the Park, the larger mammals are wary and not easily seen.

Borneo's most famous mammals are the Orang-utans, unmistakable from their size and their russet fur. Orang-utans have been recorded on Kinabalu up to 1450 metres (4,750 feet) though they are generally creatures of the lowlands. No one knows how many Orang-utans occur within the park; estimates range from 25 to 120. Like most of the larger mammals, they are encountered only in the more undisturbed parts of the Park, though in the past, sightings were more common, particularly along the Langanan waterfall trail.

Other primates in the Park include the Grey and Maroon Langurs, the Long-tailed and Pig-tailed Macaques, the Bornean Gibbon, the Tarsier and the Slow Loris. All these are mainly lowland residents, though the Maroon Langur has been recorded at over 3,000 metres (9,800 feet) along the Summit Trail and one group regularly visits the Mesilau Nature Resort at 2,000 metres (6,500 feet). All have also been recorded at the Poring Hot Springs in the past, but there have been only occasional sightings in recent years.

A relatively recent record of some interest is that of a solitary Proboscis Monkey from the riverine forest near Serinsim on the north-eastern boundary of the park, far from the mangrove forests that are its normal home.

Other large mammals recorded from the mountain include deer, Bearded Pig and the Honey Bear. Again, though mainly found in the lowland forest on the Park's eastern and northern boundaries, stray individuals of both Sambar Deer and Barking Deer have been reliably reported as high as 3,350 metres (11,000 feet). Wild pigs used to be common on the mountain ridges up to 2,450 metres, (8,000 feet) where they built their 'nests' in thickets of orchids and ferns during the breeding season. The highest record for the Honey Bear is similar, at 2,300 metres(7,500 feet) on the Summit Trail several years ago. This, again, was probably a stray individual, wandering far from its usual range.

Squirrels and tree-shrews are undoubtedly the easiest mammals to see, being active during the day. Superficially tree-shrews and squirrels look alike, but the squirrels are mainly tree dwellers, while the tree-shrews forage mainly on the ground or in low bushes. They are easy to distinguish from the squirrels by their longer, more pointed noses. In the lowland forest, the Common Tree-shrew *(Tupaia glis)* is the most abundant, and it is thought to be a dispersal agent for the parasitic Rafflesia. In the mountain forest it is replaced by the Mountain Tree-shrew (*Tupaia montana)*.

Squirrels are almost as easily seen, ranging from the tiny Whitehead's Pygmy Squirrel (*Exilisciurus whiteheadii*) nibbling mosses and tree-bark in the hill dipterocarp forest and above, to the Giant Tree-squirrel, (*Ratufa affinis*), the size of a cat, that reaches the upper parts of its range around Park HQ. The Bornean Mountain Ground Squirrel (*Dremomys everetti*), with an unusually pointed nose for a squirrel, is almost as common as the Mountain Tree-shrew from Park HQ up to 3,400 metres (11,000 feet) but can be distinguished by its shorter, bushier tail.

*Slow Loris*

# Trails, Climbs and other Attractions

The Park's system of trails allows visitors to make the most of their visit, with trails ranging from less than half an hour to four days in length.

The wide altitudinal range covered by the park means that a large number of different habitats and forest types are found within its environs. Nowhere else in the world is it possible, in the space of a single day, to go from the pristine lowland dipterocarp forests (such as those found at Poring), into the montane oak-chestnut forest (surrounding Park HQ and Mesilau), past open, grassy sub-alpine meadows (found at the edge of the tree-line on Kinabalu) and finally up onto the bare summit slabs where the only plants that can survive are a few tough sedges or grasses or stunted bonsai-like shrubs in sheltered crevices. Each trail offers something different, and the trail network as a whole allows full exploration of this unique natural environment.

# Around Headquarters

## THE ROAD UP

The HQ of the Kinabalu Park lies at an elevation of 1,563 metres (5,128 feet) on the Park's southern boundary. The 80 kilometre (50 mile) drive along a sealed road takes an easy two hours from Kota Kinabalu, the capital of Sabah, but not until the road passes the little town of Tamparuli, after about 40 minutes, does it start to rise. Secondary scrub, bananas and the occasional fruit tree are interspersed with rubber trees grown by smallholders on the lower slopes and introduced softwood acacias are planted along much of the roadside, though many trees were burnt during the drought in 1998. Under the acacia trees, the burnt ground is covered in the thorny sensitive plant *Mimosa pudica* with its feathery leaves that close at the touch of a finger, while in more open areas sun loving ferns clad the banks.

Although clouds usually cover the summit by midday, in the early morning the mountain is often clear, the view constantly changing as the road winds up and up. Some of the best views come near Kampung Kelawat at the kilometre 55 (to Ranau) mark, when the mountain rises dramatically ahead as you round a corner. A few kilometres further on the best views of a separate, much lower, peak (Gunung Sadok-Sadok) can be seen in front of the main massif, known as the *anak* or 'child' of Kinabalu which reaches only 1,800 metres (5,491 feet). Then the *kampung* of Kaung appears far down in the valley near the base of the *anak*, its tin roofs shining in the sun, and further up the *kampung* of Kiau. Both were standard stops for early climbers before any roads were built and Kiau was the last stop before the steep ascent of the mountain itself.

Shifting cultivation covers most of the hills around here, and at kilometre 33 the roadside stalls of Pekan Nabalu are well stocked with local produce. This is a regular tourist stop where a variety of good quality handicrafts can be purchased as well as the deliciously nutty flavoured brown hill rice – a speciality of the area, together with extra sweet pineapples. Many different varieties of bananas are also sold here, varying from the tiny sweet yellow *pisang mas* (*pisang* meaning banana in Bahasa Malaysia), to the larger dark red *pisang merah* and the more delicately flavoured green *pisang hijau*. Other local fruits can also be seen in season as well as wild honey sold in old beer bottles.

At kilometre 29, at the turn-off to Kampung Kiau, the air is already cooler and yellow daisies become increasingly common, scattered through the grass at the edge of the road. Above and in front lies the Tenompok Forest Reserve, much of which was burnt during the 1998 drought. Soon you pass the Kiau Nabalu restaurant on the roadside, 6 kilometres (4 miles) from the Park HQ, where there are good views of the patterned fields of shifting cultivation above the *kampung* of Kiau. If the day is clear there are also excellent views of the long trailing waterfall of the Kadamaian from here onwards to the Tenompok Pass. A rough road to the right at the pass leads down to another historic village, Bundu Tuhan, where the most famous of the mountain guides, Gunting bin Lagadan, lived, well-known as a teller of tales and legends and now the stuff of legend himself. Gunting was reputed to possess remarkable powers, including the ability to protect from evil spirits all who climbed with him, and he became the park's first officially registered guide.

At the Tenompok Pass, just after the kilometre 22 mark, you cross over to the main massif and within five minutes reach the impressive arched entrance of the Kinabalu Park HQ, with introduced pine trees and blue morning glory flowers along the roadside. There are several signboards here advertising various motels and lodges around the Park and at Kundasang.

## KINABALU PARK HEADQUARTERS

Today the Kinabalu Park is visited by well over 200,000 people a year. More than 20,000 make the 8.7 kilometre (5½ mile) climb to the summit of the mountain, a steep ascent of earth steps and wooden ladders, but one which remains basically a two day walk, rather than a climb, within the reach of anyone who is reasonably fit and healthy.

The Park HQ can sleep a total of 228 persons in a variety of accommodation types ranging from hostels with only basic facilities to more luxurious individual chalets (see **Planning and Practicalities**, page 24). An intercom system links the chalets to the reception office. Most have self-catering facilities but there are also two restaurants serving both western and oriental food. Fireplaces are provided in some chalets and firewood can be purchased from the Reception office at HQ, but it is a good idea to bring old newspaper and candles or a lighter as well as matches from KK. The Park has its own generator and electricity is provided 24 hours a day. There is a small souvenir and sundries shop and public payphones. Guided walks and audio-visual shows are presented by the interpretation staff. A nominal fee is charged for some of these programmes, as well as a fee to enter the Park.

Other facilities at Park HQ include a fitness centre and a multipurpose hall that also serves as a badminton court. Shuttlecocks must be purchased unless you bring your own, but racquets can be rented for a small fee.

From the entrance a sealed one-way road forms a loop running through the Park HQ complex that lies in the heart of the montane oak/chestnut/conifer forest. The loop road is excellent for both insects and birds. The Kinabalu Park is, in fact, probably the best place in Borneo to see montane birds such as the Ashy Drongos with

### Introduced exotics

First time visitors to the park are often pleasantly surprised by the planted beds of brightly coloured flowers. These should not be mistaken for native species however. Bright yellow day-lillies line the roadsides at the main entrance and have been planted all around the Park HQ, together with brilliant orange geraniums, pink and orange balsams, blue morning-glory and deep purple shrubby Tibouchina, this last from the tropical mountains of South America. Introduced conifers were also planted long ago around the hostels and reception buildings. The pines along the road down to Kundasang are a more recent introduction.

white eye patches and distinctive forked tails hawking for insects by the street lamps and ungainly long-tailed Bornean Treepies sounding their musical 'cloink' call. Flocks of Chestnut-capped Laughing-thrushes, often joined by white-eyes, warblers and yuhinas, often hunt through the bushes at the roadside, their laughing cackle a characteristic sound in the mountain forest.

Also commonly seen along the road here are beautiful Green Magpies, Black-and-crimson Orioles, stunning flame-coloured minivets and the gorgeous red Mountain Sunbird as well as the duller Flavescent Bulbul. Rarer birds that skulk quietly in the undergrowth are the dark Sunda Whistling Thrush that haunts the dim forest, and the Orange-headed Thrush.

During the migration season, several flycatchers stay over in the Park and the little bobbing Grey Wagtail is often seen along the roadside ditches. Whitehead's Spiderhunter, streaked distinctive brown and white, often visits epiphytic rhododendrons high in the trees, while one of Kinabalu's most beautiful birds, the brilliant green Whitehead's Broadbill, is occasionally seen or heard growling in the mist along the road. The equally beautiful grey and red Whitehead's Trogon prefers more undisturbed forest along the trails.

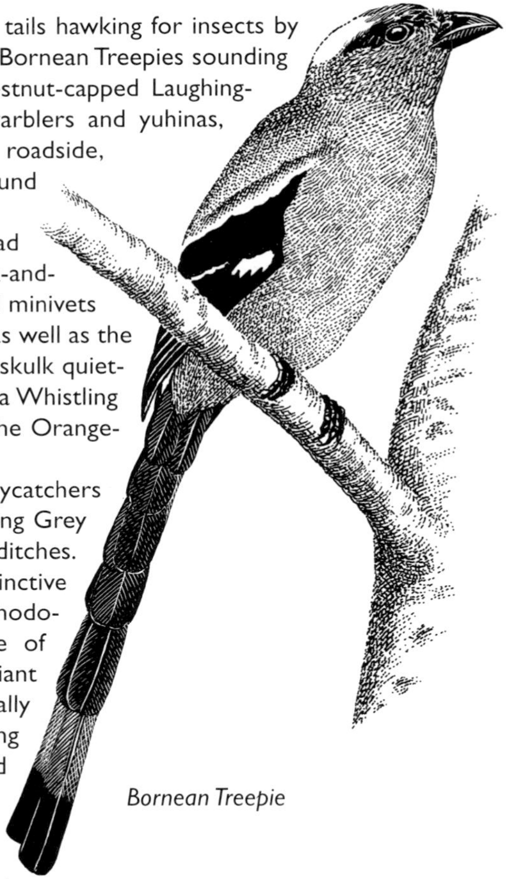

*Bornean Treepie*

From time to time small groups of the rare but lovely grey-and-black Black-breasted Fruit-hunters and the much duller Black Laughing-thrushes fly in for a few days before disappearing to another part of the mountain, not to be seen at the HQ again for months.

## THE POWER STATION ROAD

The Power Station road is basically an extension of the loop through the Park HQ. It is particularly rewarding for birdwatchers, especially in the early morning or evening. Many interesting plants which are not found in the closed forest grow in open areas along the roadside or on rocky banks.

The Power Station at the end of the road provides electricity for the government run radio and TV transmitter aerials higher up the mountain. Climbers usually get a lift from Park Headquarters to the Power Station and the Timpohon Gate at 1,866 metres (1,622 feet) where the Summit Trail starts, but the steeply ascending 4 kilometre (2½ mile) sealed road is well worth a walk, especially if you get a lift up and walk down.

Around the Park HQ complex the road is lined with stately tree-ferns, but further up, past all the street lights and buildings, seedlings of native conifers have been planted. Both the ridge-top Kiau View Trail and the stream-side Silau–Silau Trail emerge onto the Power Station road opposite each other a little further up, thus making these walks easy to combine. Even further up is the entrance to the ridge-top Mempening Trail which joins the Bukit Tupai/Bukit Burong section, and one can return to Park HQ by this route also.

The open grassy verges along the roadside support a number of especially sun loving plants. Ferns such as *Dipteris* with shiny reddish circular fronds and the common *Blechnum*, with large coarse fronds, pinkish when young, grow with dense thickets of *Gleichenia*, a tropical bracken-like fern with slender forking fronds. The wild shrub raspberry (*Rubus fraxinifolius*) growing amongst them has conspicuous loose bunches of dry, sour red fruits, that are so covered with pips that they look more like strawberries.

A conspicuous sun loving orchid on the steep banks here is the Yellow Buttercup Orchid (*Spathoglottis microcheilina*) with long, soft, pleated leaves. Tall clumps of Bamboo Orchids (*Arundina bambusifolia*) with purple and white flowers line the ditches; sometimes a peculiar variant with all white flowers can be seen.

Grasshoppers and green-and-gold spiders are numerous among the grasses along the verge, which are often white with dew on the pocket-handkerchief webs of the spiders in the early morning. Other roadside shrubs include the mountain *Melastoma* with its large pale pinkish flowers and *Mussaenda* which has startling white bracts to set off its small orange flowers.

About halfway up the road, just after the kilometre 2.5 mark, lies the Kiau Gap – an open pass across the ridge from the west coast to the Liwagu valley on the eastern side of Kinabalu. This place has superb views of the cascading Kadamaian waterfall, with the bare rock scar to the left caused by 1994 tropical storm Greg – Sabah's worst storm in living memory – and past Gunung Sadok-Sadok (the *anak* or 'child' of Kinabalu) west down to the coast.

The Gap is an excellent place for butterflies. Few butterflies occur above 2,000 metres (6,500 feet) on Kinabalu but normally lowland species can often be seen here, windblown up the valley. They do not go higher up the mountain. The few species that do regularly fly higher include some in the cabbage-white family (Pieriidae), which are well-known for their extensive migrations. Great numbers of these can occasionally be seen being blown over the Kiau Gap and down the Liwagu valley like large pale-yellow snowflakes. If you are lucky you might also see a flock of Wreathed Hornbills flying above the canopy across the Gap. This is the only hornbill species you are likely to see at this elevation – but always in passing.

Rhododendrons flower seasonally in the shrubbery on the high roadside banks. Largest is the "showpiece" Kinabalu rhododendron with handsome heads of rich orangy-pink flowers with yellow throats, which may rise startlingly amid a thicket of thin climbing bamboos and bracken. This is *Rhododendron brookeanum*, another of Low's discoveries, named after his good friend, the Rajah Brooke of Sarawak. A smaller plant, *R.suaveolens*, has clusters of delicate pure white flowers, while *R.polyanthemum*, with tight clusters of sweetly scented small orange flowers, appears on exposed cliffs near the Power Station itself.

## MOUNTAIN GARDEN

One of the biggest attractions at the Park HQ is the Mountain Garden, a showcase of the diversity of plant life on the mountain, which was started in 1981. Plants from all over the Park are grown here in natural surroundings. Many are labelled and many also have traditional uses within the Dusun community. The fenced site covers roughly 2 hectares (5 acres), straddling the Silau-Silau stream, just below the old Administration building. Gravelled, well graded paths lead visitors through plant display houses as well as enriched forest. Knowledgeable Park guides take groups round the garden at certain times only. Check with the Park Administration on arrival for these times. A nominal fee is charged for these walks.

Interesting small trees in the Mountain Garden include the Kinabalu Nutmeg (*Knema kinabaluensis*), the Kerosene tree (*Pittosporum resiniferum*) and the Earth Fig (*Ficus uncinata*). Kinabalu has a richer fig flora than any other area of comparable size in the world. At least 78 of Borneo's 135 figs are recorded from the mountain, varying from the giant stranglers of the lowland forest to tiny dwarf bushes rooted in rock cracks above 3,000 metres (10,000 feet). Many figs exhibit the phenomenon of cauliflory, with clusters of fruits dangling from their branches or gathered in a stringy skirt around the base of the trunk which exude a sticky white latex if picked when unripe. Some even produce fruit on long trailing runners buried in the leaf-litter. The latter are known as "earth" figs and *F. uncinata* belongs in this group. It is easily recognised by this habit and by its scaly red fruits, often half nibbled by squirrels.

The nutmeg, its shiny dark seeds enclosed in a glistening crimson aril, does not have the fragrance and spice of the commercial species, but is well-liked by birds. The Kerosene tree has fat round bunches of small orange fruits clustering along its branches. The fruits are full of a clear, sticky oil (up to 15% by weight), which can be squeezed out of the fruit and ignited. In hard times in the past, before kerosene became available, the oil was sometimes used for lamps by the local people.

Climbing up these little trees, and sometimes covering the crowns, are *Bauhinia* lianas with large flowers that open white, turning yellow on the second day, and distinctive "twin" leaves like a butterfly or goat's foot, while in damp patches along the streams grows the lovely pink-flowered Kinabalu Balsam. Ferns are also abundant, two of the more interesting being the primitive *Angiopteris*,

### Wasps and figs

Fig flowers and fruits are among the strangest in the plant kingdom. The minute flowers, small as pinheads, are produced inside the fruit, which is turned inside-out, as it were, and are pollinated by tiny wasps, different species for each kind of fig. Figs have three sorts of flowers – male, female and neuter. The wasps lay their eggs in the neuter flowers which develop into galls, providing food for the larvae. When these hatch, the wasps carry the pollen of the male flowers with them through the narrow opening to the outside world and transfer it to female flowers in the other figs they enter to lay their eggs, so start the cycle again.

KINABALU'S RENOWNED BIOLOGICAL DIVERSITY IS DETERMINED BY MANY FACTORS, INCLUDING SOIL, TEMPERATURE, RAINFALL AND EXPOSURE.

ABOVE: THE GREY-TAILED RACER IS A NON VENOMOUS PREDATOR OF BIRDS AND RODENTS.

RIGHT: THE ABUNDANT BORNEAN MOUNTAIN GROUND SQUIRREL IS FOUND ON ALL OF BORNEO'S HIGHER MOUNTAINS.

BELOW RIGHT: THE CAMOUFLAGE OF THE HORNED TOAD RENDERS IT ALMOST INVISIBLE AGAINST THE FOREST FLOOR.

OPPOSITE TOP: THE NOISY RHINOCEROS HORNBILL IS FOUND IN THE FOREST CANOPY.

OPPOSITE BOTTOM LEFT: THE MALE THREE-HORNED RHINOCEROS BEETLE USES ITS IMRESSIVE APPENDAGES IN TERRITORIAL COMBAT.

OPPOSITE BOTTOM RIGHT: THE LEOPARD CAT IS A RESIDENT OF THE LOWLAND FOREST, BY NATURE SECRETIVE AND NOCTURNAL, SO SELDOM SEEN.

ABOVE: STREAMSIDE TRAILS ARE LINED WITH AN ABUNDANCE OF SHADE AND DAMP LOVING SPECIES SUCH AS FERNS, GINGERS AND AROIDS,

with huge fronds rather like those of a tree fern, but lacking a trunk and the little Snake's Tongue fern, *Ophioglossum*, with simple sterile smooth leaves, the spores produced on a separate fertile spike. In damp places by the little stream wending its way through the plant houses, a cousin of the ferns, the tropical mountain horsetail, *Equisetum ramossisimum* has been planted, its upright spikes bearing small black club-like heads. Climbing rattan palms grow in open spaces at the edge of the trail, their thorny flexible stems sprawling across the ground - look out for the thorny leaf-tips as you walk. Lowland rattans are a major forest product, used to make cane furniture that is exported worldwide. The mountain species are fewer and their stems lack the length and strength of the lowland species, but they are used by the local people for handicrafts and as twine.

Other interesting plant groups include wild bananas, aroids, climbing bamboos, several species of lipstick flowers (*Aeschynanthus* spp.) and various species of *Medinella* which are undoubtedly the most startling of all the plants of the lower montane forest, with eye-catching bunches of pink or white flowers. One species, *Medinella speciosa* with large trusses of bright pink flowers followed by dark purple-black berries is planted extensively around the Park HQ. This is also the commonest species in the Mountain Garden but several others grow as scrambling shrubs or climbers. When nothing else seems to be in flower, usually a *Medinella* can be found here and there, lighting up the forest gloom.

Of the lipstick flowers there are three common species in the park and all grow in the Mountain Garden. The bright scarlet corollas of Miss Gibb's Lipstick Flower (*Aeschynanthus gibbsiae*) contrast with the bright green calices, both covered in a soft down. *A. magnifica* has duller purple flowers, but the loveliest of all is *A. speciosus* with gorgeous yellow, black and red colouring that stands out in the forest shade.

Gingers are some of the showiest flowers on Kinabalu, though they often bloom close to the ground and may be overshadowed by their leaves. These gingers belong to the same family as the commercially cultivated ginger spice but only one of the wild species in Borneo seems to have any sort of commercial importance. This is the massive-leaved *tuhau* (*Etlingera punicea*), a lowland species, whose fronds can reach three metres (ten feet) in length. The brilliant red and yellow flowers are produced in small clusters on the ground. The young stems, which have a distinctive pungent smell, are peeled, chopped up and mixed with chilli and garlic to make a sort of relish that is used widely by the local people in Sabah. This relish can often be seen for sale in old coffee jars on roadside or market stalls.

*Etlingera muluensis*, which does grows in the Mountain Garden, is very similar in habit but its flowers are smaller and borne in compact bunches on short, stout, dark-red stalks at the base of the plant, above the leaf-litter. Other gingers in the Mountain Garden are very different in their lifestyle. One of the commonest is *Hedychium cylindricum*. This rarely reaches more than a metre (three feet) in height and bears its erect spikes of white butterfly-like flowers, followed by brilliant orange-red fruits, at the top of its short fronds. Another common Kinabalu species, *Alpinia havilandii*, has fronds only slightly taller with tubular white and red flowers carried in short bunches about a third of the way up the stem, just below the first leaves, while *Amomum kinabaluen-*

*sis*, growing in compact bushy clumps not taller than a metre (three feet), has large golden flowers half buried in the leaf-litter. Another common ginger, *Hornstedtia incana*, has a fat spindle shaped inflorescence with bright waxy-red or pink flowers like a duck's bill produced on short stilt roots around the base of the plant. The related *Hornstedtia gracilis* has unusually tall and narrow spindle-inflorescences.

*Orchids*

It is for its variety of orchids that the mountain is best known, and justly so. The mountain is a treasure-trove of orchid diversity, containing representatives from all the five sub-families, and is particularly rich in the more primitive orchids. Orchids have exerted a fascination over man for centuries. The Chinese were probably the first to cultivate them, for their fragrance, but in the 19th century they were a symbol of wealth among the European aristocracy with rare plants changing hands for hundreds of pounds – a small fortune in those days. Some of the rarest came from Kinabalu. One of these was once described as the noblest of all orchids, *Paphiopedilum rothschildianum* or Rothschild's slipper orchid, found only on Mount Kinabalu. Its sweeping petals, some 12cm (4½ inches) across, resemble the outspread arms of a Dusun girl performing the traditional *sumazau* dance.

The best time to see flowering orchids at the Park HQ is November to February, during the rains, but there will always be some in flower, though you may have to look carefully to see them. May to June is also usually quite good for flowering.

Some of the most spectacular are the necklace orchids (*Coelogyne* spp) dangling their long trailing blooms from the tree branches, their large white flowers ridged or marked with chocolate or yellow on the lip. *Chelonistele* orchids, on the other hand, which are almost as attractive, have upright spikes of scented brownish-cream flowers. Orchids in the genus *Bulbophyllum* are also very common but many are so small they can easily be missed, with tiny yellow or purple flowers growing on mossy tree-trunks. Then there are the ground dwelling *Calanthe* orchids with their fat golden upright heads of flowers poking up from the leaf litter; the Mountain slipper orchid *Paphiopedilum javanicum* with its curiously

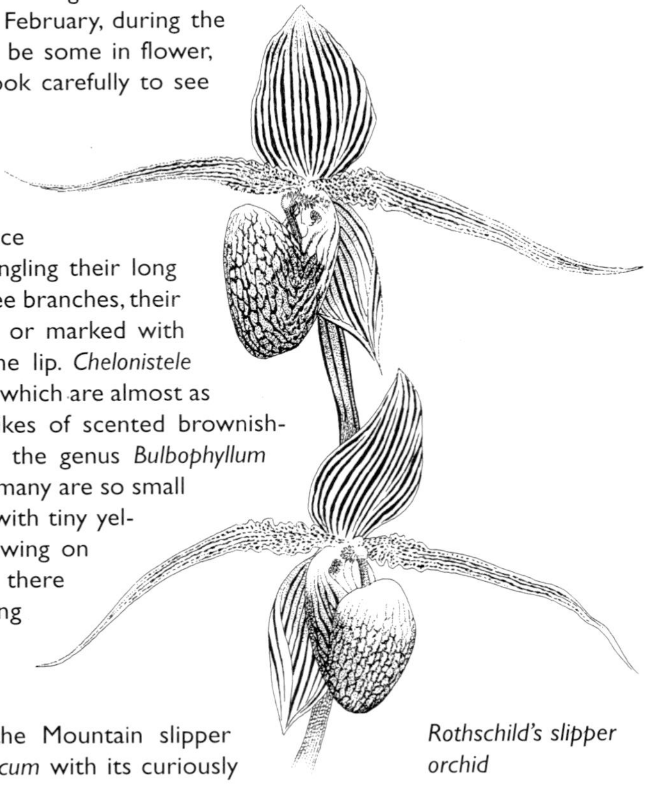

*Rothschild's slipper orchid*

## Orchid flowers

Although they differ greatly in appearance, every orchid flower has the same structure of three sepals and three petals. Two of the petals are usually very similar to the sepals, but the third petal, called the 'lip', is always distinctive and serves as a landing platform to lure pollinating insects to the staminode in the heart of the flower. Sometimes the flower of an orchid may be difficult to see, but a closer look, perhaps even with a magnifying glass, will reveal an amazing complexity and delicacy of detail in even the smallest.

pouched lip; *Liparis* with double rows of bright orange flowers; *Cymbidium* with strings of dark purple flowers half-hidden among its long narrow leaves; the Helmet orchid, *Corybas*, with its beautifully veined, heart shaped leaves and curious cup-like flowers nestled into the mossy banks; and a hundred others with flowers that range from the size of a pinhead to huge trusses up to a metre (three feet) or more in length. Some of the smallest in the world are the tiny white-flowered *Podochilus* orchids that clad the treetrunks like thick ferns, while the equally small-flowered Ribbon orchid (*Taeniophyllum*) has no leaves at all, making do with flat green roots clinging to the branches instead.

The leaves of other orchids vary from long and sword-like to broad and fat, some with a swollen base (called a pseudobulb) that is used to store water and starch in times of drought. In other orchids the whole leaf may be thick and succulent, or thin and pliant. Some saprophytic ground orchids have no leaves at all, getting their nutrients entirely from decaying leaves on the forest floor.

Two particularly rare species found wild in the mountain garden are the saprophytic *Pantlingia lamrii* (named after the Director of Sabah Parks, Datuk Lamri Ali), with its delicate jade-green flowers and the more robust *Hylophila lanceolata*, with stout spikes of pinky-orange flowers. Some of the loveliest species of all are the dainty jewel orchids of the forest floor – *Anoectochilus*, its dark chocolate-brown leaves veined with gold, and *Kuhlhasseltia*, its leaves lined with black velvet.

Most orchids have specific pollinators that are attracted by a variety of mechanisms. Scent (sweet or foul), reward, traps, deceit and mimicry are all employed to ensure the next generation. In Rothschild's slipper orchid, part of the flower mimics an aphid colony and is pollinated by syrphid flies who normally lay their eggs in such colonies. In other species, the flowers mimic the females of certain bees so well that they are pollinated by male bees in their attempts to copulate. Yet other species resort to physical force, possessing a 'lip' that is so delicately balanced it catapults the insect into the heart of the flower as soon as it lands. In its struggle to escape, pollination ensues. The white moth-pollinated flowers of many orchids exude a sweet fragrance to attract their pollinators while the purple-spotted flowers of carrion-smelling species exude an overpowering smell of rotting meat, attracting blue-bottle flies as pollinators. Nectar is offered as a reward by many orchids and a few that are pollinated by fruit flies provide essential chemicals that the flies need to make them distasteful to potential predators.

# Headquarters Trails

The forest around the Kinabalu Park Headquarters is always beautiful, whether it is lit by the first rays of the sun over the eastern ridge, shadowed by passing clouds at midday or veiled in drifting mists at evening. Squirrels and tree shrews scramble in the thickets and birds call in the canopy overhead. In the early morning mist and evening rain can be heard the mournful call of the Little Cuckoo-dove. Even in the middle of the day the monotonous "took-took-terrook" of the Golden-naped Barbet echoes far and wide over mountain and valley. Cicadas zither and hum off and on throughout the day and the wind murmuring in the tree tops brings the cool air of the higher mountain to refresh the weary visitor from the enervating heat of the lowlands. Strange and beautiful fungi grow on tree roots in the moss or on fallen mossy branches, while the primeval looking trilobite beetles sway through miniature forests of moss growing on rotting logs. There is always something of interest along these paths and a number of walking trails have been developed around the Park HQ ranging in length from 20 minutes to two or three hours. These trails are marked on the trail maps available at Park HQ. Remember that times given are approximate and vary greatly depending on how fit you are and how often you stop.

The trails around headquarters can be divided into two basic groups – ridgetop trails and streamside trails.

## RIDGETOP TRAILS

### Kiau View Trail (c.90 minutes one way)

This starts by the entrance arch into the Kinabalu Park and comes out just after the 1.5 kilometre (1 mile) mark on the Power Station road opposite the entrance to the Silau-Silau Trail. A wide undulating ridge trail with several shelters and good views looking down to the west coast, it is excellent for familiarising yourself with the most typical trees of Kinabalu's mountain forest.

### Pandanus Trail (c. 20 minutes to Kiau View trail)

This trail was completed only recently as part of the route for the World Mountain Running Trophy Race that took place at the Kinabalu Park in September 1999. As a result the trail is broad and well graded. It starts just opposite the entrance to the car park at the Administration Building, zigzagging up the side of the ridge to reach the Kiau View Trail at the ridge crest.

### Bukit Ular Hillside Trail (c. 30 minutes)

A fairly steep trail that contours around the side of Bukit Ular near the top end of the Power Station road. It starts about two-thirds of the way up the Power Station road coming out just behind the Power Station itself. A steep 30 minute detour just below the Power Station leads to the top of Bukit Ular with excellent waterfall and mountain views.

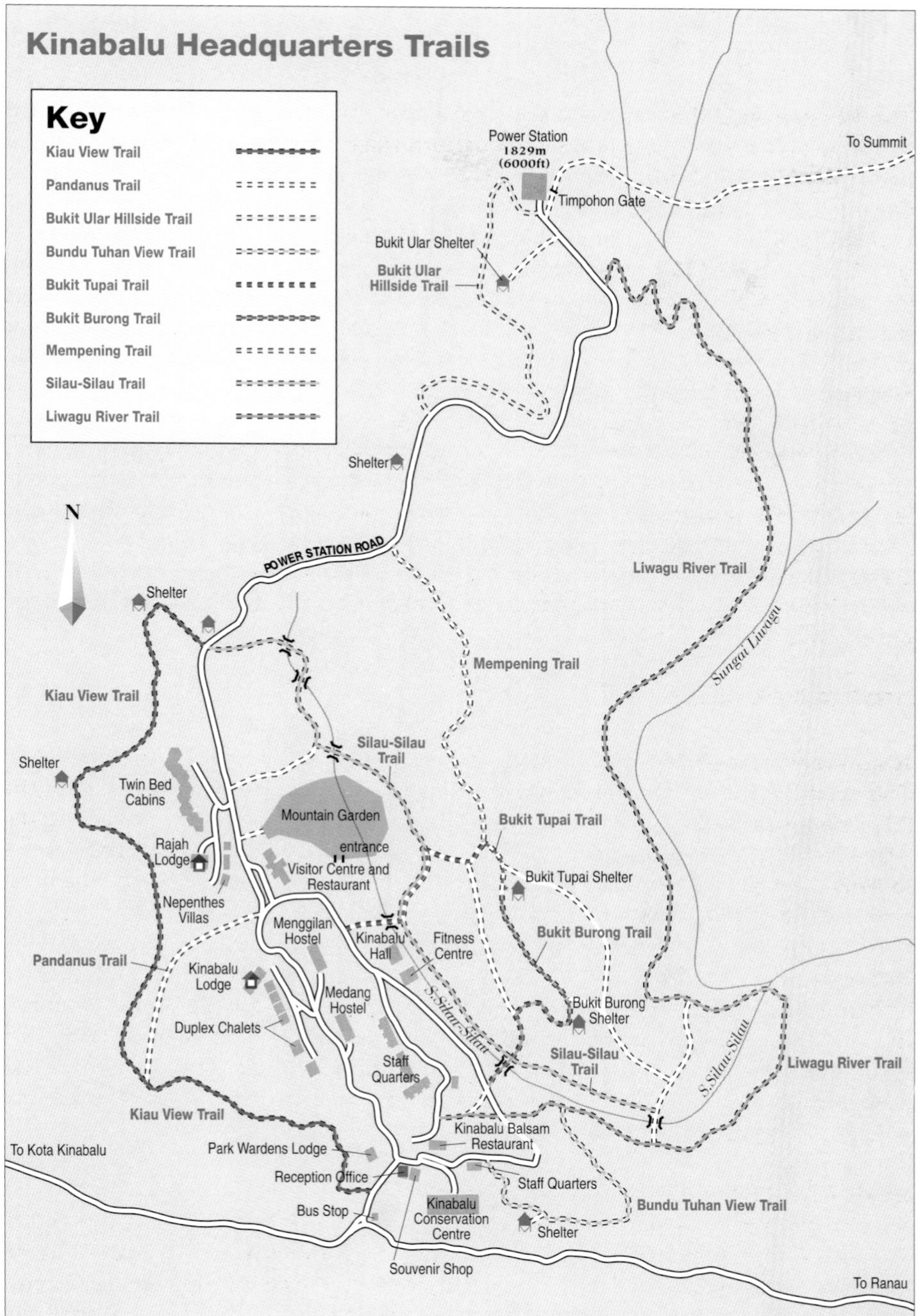
Kinabalu Headquarters Trails
Key
Kiau View Trail
Pandanus Trail
Bukit Ular Hillside Trail
Bundu Tuhan View Trail
Bukit Tupai Trail
Bukit Burong Trail
Mempening Trail
Silau-Silau Trail
Liwagu River Trail
N
Power Station
1829m
(6000ft)
To Summit
Timpohon Gate
Bukit Ular Shelter
Bukit Ular
Hillside Trail
Shelter
POWER STATION ROAD
Shelter
Liwagu River Trail
Sungai Liwagu
Mempening Trail
Kiau View Trail
Shelter
Silau-Silau
Trail
Twin Bed
Cabins
Mountain Garden
Bukit Tupai Trail
entrance
Rajah
Lodge
Visitor Centre and
Restaurant
Bukit Tupai Shelter
Nepenthes
Villas
Menggilan
Hostel
Kinabalu
Hall
Fitness
Centre
Bukit Burong Trail
Pandanus Trail
Kinabalu
Lodge
S. Silau-Silau
Medang
Hostel
Bukit Burong
Shelter
Duplex Chalets
Staff
Quarters
Silau-Silau
Trail
S. Silau-Silau
Liwagu River Trail
Kiau View Trail
Kinabalu Balsam
Restaurant
To Kota Kinabalu
Park Wardens Lodge
Reception Office
Staff Quarters
Bundu Tuhan View Trail
Bus Stop
Kinabalu
Conservation
Centre
Shelter
Souvenir Shop
To Ranau

**Bundu Tuhan View Trail (7 minutes to the ridgetop shelter; 25 minutes to Liwagu Trail)**
Starts from the loop road below the staff quarters near the Conservation Centre. The trail leads up to a shelter on top of the ridge above the main highway to Ranau which gives good views of Bundu Tuhan village and a panorama of the southern mountains, including Trus Madi (2642m), the second highest peak in Sabah. Then continue down the side of the ridge to the Liwagu Trail.

**Bukit Tupai Trail (25 minutes)**
A short trail that starts near the Multipurpose Hall, crosses the Silau-Silau stream and trail and goes straight up to the ridge crest and the Bukit Tupai shelter. Excellent views of the HQ complex, the tree canopy and in clear weather outstanding views of Mt. Kinabalu. At the ridge crest it joins the Mempening and Bukit Burong trails.

**Bukit Burong Trail (10 minutes to Silau-Silau, 25 mins to Bukit Burong)**
Starts from the road, first crossing the Silau-silau stream and trail, then going gradually up the ridge side to the Bukit Burong shelter at the top. The trail connects to the Mempening Trail via the Bukit Tupai shelter. They are favourites with visitors because of the variety and convenience, combining hill forest, cool stream valley and dry ridge tops. Bukit Burong shelter gives fine panoramas of Kinabalu, the lower Liwagu valley and the HQ area.

**Mempening Trail (30 minutes from road to Silau-Silau)**
Another ridgetop trail starting about halfway up the Power Station road and leading down the ridge through dense oak-chestnut forest to Bukit Tupai and the Silau Silau stream. Good views of the Park HQ complex and the Liwagu valley.

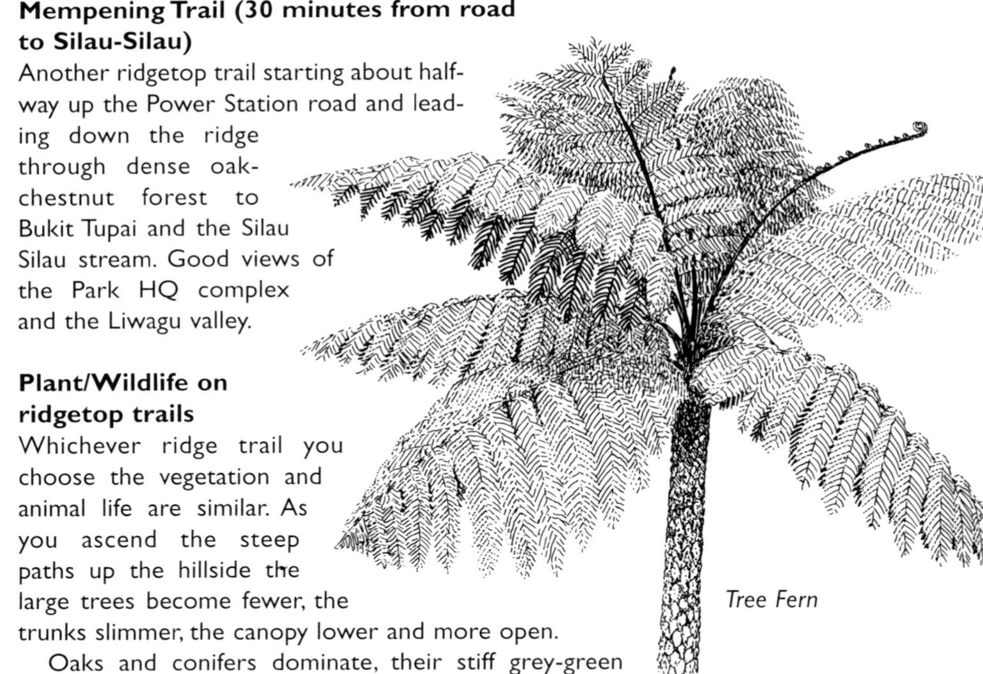
*Tree Fern*

**Plant/Wildlife on ridgetop trails**
Whichever ridge trail you choose the vegetation and animal life are similar. As you ascend the steep paths up the hillside the large trees become fewer, the trunks slimmer, the canopy lower and more open.

Oaks and conifers dominate, their stiff grey-green

leaves and spikes of dusty yellow blossom lighting up the canopy in season.

One of the most peculiar is the Trig Oak which starts by developing a big trunk, then sends up numerous side-shoots from the main trunk which rots away, leaving the side shoots developing into a cluster of sturdy young trunks. Some of the oldest trees have a hollow bole a metre or more (several feet) across with a thicket of secondary trunks fencing it around. The Trig Oak was first discovered on Kinabalu during the Royal Society Expedition in 1961 and hailed as a living fossil link between the oaks, chestnuts and beeches of cooler climes – thus its cumbersome Latin name *Trigonobalanus verticellatus*, and so, Trig Oak. With its whorled leaves and clusters of tiny triangular beech nut like fruits, this tree is distinctive and quite common around the Park HQ.

Of the southern hemisphere conifers, which with the oaks dominate the canopy at this height, the grandest is *Agathis*, a relative of the New Zealand Kauri Pine whose splendid columnar trunk soars up into a spiky crown of stiff leaves and flaky dappled bark which secretes a thick white aromatic resin, the "dammar" of former commerce. Trees near Park HQ often bear old wounds and galls caused by local tappers in the past.

In contrast *Dacrycarpus imbricatus* conifers have grey shaggy trunks and large spreading crowns of graceful grey-green cypressy foliage; their seedlings bear delicate needle twigs like little combs. Their scarlet berry-like seeds on green pedestals are very popular with barbets and other canopy birds. The other common conifer at this height, *Dacrydium beccarii*, has thicker green needle twigs, its ascending branches spreading out in layers into a flattened umbrella crown forming gnarled, crooked shapes on exposed ridges.

Where ridge tops bear a good covering of trees the ground is often covered with a carpet of moss, and mosses also cover the trunks and on steep slopes the exposed roots of trees where the soil has been eroded to form small caves between the roots. All sorts of weird and beautiful fungi flourish in the litter and on exposed roots. Among them may be found small red or yellow *Balanophora* parasites. These are flowering plants, not fungi and occur in colonies with male and female plants, the female being a tight thumb-sized head of minute flowerets, the male a spike of larger but fewer flowers with white pollen enclosed in fleshy bracts. They develop at certain seasons from coral-like tubers buried in the litter. The bright pink *Balanophora reflexa* is the most common species.

Another parasite on oak roots is the little *Mitrastemmon* which no-one would ever guess is in the same family as the spectacular Rafflesia. In the Kinabalu Park this tiny little cream-coloured flower surrounded by a few fleshy-pink bracts has so far only ever been found on one spot along the Bukit Tupai-Bukit Burong Trail, but it is also recorded from as far away as Japan. Also on the mossy ridges one sometimes sees the smallest of the Kinabalu pitcher plants, *Nepenthes tentaculata*, with green and reddish pitchers, many with a fringe of filaments round the lid.

The ridge top, exposed to more light, is a favourite spot for some ground rhododendrons like *Rhododendron gracile* with large pale yellow flowers and the tiny *R.borneensis* whose minute, red tube flowers occur in tangled shrubs of very small leaves, either on the ground or lodged in low trees. Here also grows *Drimys piperita* with small white flowers. This shrub is one of the most primitive of all the flowering plants, and a true montane forest indicator, growing as its does between 1,200 and 1,500 metres (4,000 and 5,000 feet).

The ridgetop shelters of Bukit Burong and Bukit Tupai are a good place to look for birds in the early morning or evening. The little Jentinck's Squirrel (*Sundasciurus jentincki*), one of the commonest species around Park HQ, with its conspicuous white eye ring and white ear edging, is often seen at these times.

Despite the cold, a few snakes do occur at Park HQ and above – the Speckle-bellied Keelback (*Rhabdorphis chrysarga*) may be curled up for warmth in a sunny patch at the trail edge, or a green Pit viper (*Trimeresurus* sp) might be coiled round a slender twig, but such occasions are rare.

Some of the finest views of the higher mountain forest are from these ridgetops, looking down into the valley and up to the spurs and ridges of the middle mountain all clothed in a mantle of tree tops in a harmony of greens, greys and browns, Bright pink leaf flushes of tree bilberries (*Vaccinium* spp) here and there glow in the early sun, and glimpses of silver or scurfy gold from other trees with young leaf flushes add splashes of colour.

## STREAM-SIDE TRAILS

### Silau-Silau Trail (c.50 minutes from Power Station road to Liwagu River)

This follows the cool and mossy Silau-Silau stream for nearly all its course from its source below the Kiau Gap right down to the junction with the Liwagu river near the overhanging rock of the Liwagu Cave. Many visitors enjoy walking this trail in conjunction with another one such as Bukit Burong or Kiau View. A detour joining the Bukit Tupai Trail is made in one area to avoid the Mountain Garden. Short cuts back to the road can be taken near the twin-bed cabins and where the path joins the Bukit Tupai and Bukit Burong trails.

### Liwagu River Trail (3 hours from Power Station down to Silau-Silau junction)

The Liwagu Trail starts near the Kinabalu Balsam restaurant at Park HQ and leads down to the Silau-Silau stream but does not cross it until the junction with the Liwagu river. From here the trail follows the Liwagu river upwards, sometimes almost along the river bank, at other times on a high bluff, until it joins the Power Station road near the Timpohon Gate. This is a varied trail with ridge forest, cool stream valley, feathery rattan palms and the deep green gorge of the Liwagu itself. The trail is steep and narrow in places but there are several plants not found on other trails.

The best way to walk it is to get a lift to the Power Station and then follow the Liwagu Trail down. Because of its length the trail it is not much used and visitors should check to see if there have been any tree falls or landslides recently.

### Plant/Wildlife on stream side trails

Because it is less walked than the other trails the Liwagu River Trail is also one of the best places to see wildlife. Birdwatching is particularly good at the lower end, where

Whitehead's Trogon has been reported. Tracks of Barking Deer and Wild Pig have been seen along the lower parts of the trail, while Maroon Langurs have been spotted near the upper end. Smaller mammals are not uncommon along these trails and the quiet and patient visitor has a good chance of coming across them. Near the junction with the Silau-Silau stream, both the Malay Weasel and the Yellow-throated Marten have been observed coming down to drink, while the lovely Giant Tree-squirrel can sometimes be seen looking down from a high branch. Other squirrels commonly seen in the canopy here include Jentinck's, with its distinctive white eye-ring, and Brooke's, similar in colour but lacking the eye-ring.

In general the trees along the stream-side trails are taller than those on the ridges and it is difficult to distinguish individual trees except by their bark and fallen twigs, leaves and fruits. The most striking by far are the smooth bright orange trunks of *Tristaniopsis*, related to the Australian eucalypts or gum trees, whose peeling bark lies heaped up around the bole; they stand out glowing amid the dim grey-greens of the surrounding forest. Local legend says that the other forest trees were jealous of the beauty of the *Tristaniopsis*, because it could change its peeling bark-cloth garments keeping its trunk smooth and shining. So they knocked and hit the branches to make them twisted and crooked.

Other large trees include *Palaquium* or *nyatoh* with shaggy bark and big golden-sided leaves. The thick white latex in the bark provided the *gutta percha* of commerce from the middle of the last century when it was used to coat telephone cables being laid across the Atlantic, before *Hevea* rubber trees were discovered in Brazil.

Many of the trees bear epiphytic plants, invisible on their branches overhead, but revealing their presence by fallen leaves or flowers on the path; these may be the twin butterfly leaves or yellow lily-like flowers of the *Bauhinia* lianas, the small red or pink tubular flowers of tropical mistletoes, the bell-shaped orange-pinky flowers of *Rhododendron crassifolium* or long, mauve, tubular flowers of *R. praetervisum*.

Between the tall trees the ground is often covered with a dense, impenetrable thicket of large thorny pandans and climbing rattan palms with spiny whip-like tips to their leaves, that trap the unwary passer-by. Infinite varieties of beautiful mosses and liverworts cover the bank above the path, including the largest of all, *Dawsonia*, reaching almost a metre (three feet) in height and the umbrella-like *Hypnodendron* in damper places. *Podochilus* orchids with tiny match-head flowers are almost hidden in the mossy bark on the trees while other little flowers on the trail side bloom like jewels in the moss – shy purple or white violets, little sonerilas with three pink petals and clusters of the white ghost flower *Argostemma* and the pink four-petalled *Phyllagathis*.

Fallen on the path at different times of the year are various flowers and fruits. Wild mangosteens and magnolias, nutmegs, small shuttlecock fruits of rare hill dipterocarps, the pear-shaped orange fruits of *Dysoxylon* with their three black seeds, white saucer flowers of *Schima* and dark crimson fruits of *Ternstroemia* (both members of the tea family). There are many kinds of acorns of strange shapes and sizes. A few are rather like the acorns of the European oak *Quercus*, while others belonging to the tropical oak genus *Lithocarpus*, which dominates the mountain forest, are literally hard as stones as the Latin name suggests.

# THE SUMMIT TRAIL

The Summit climb takes at least two days. Most climbers arrive at the Park HQ the night before and start at 0700 or 0800 the next morning. A guide is compulsory for every climbing group and porters can be booked if required, as can transport to the starting point of the climb at Timpohon Gate (1,866 metres/6,122 feet), 5.5 kilometres (3 miles) from the Park Entrance.

The ascent is not difficult in climbing terms, but it is very strenuous, especially for those who are not very fit. Those who suffer from asthma, respiratory ailments, high blood pressure or heart problems should consult their doctor before attempting the climb. Most people suffer mild headaches or disorientation at Panar Laban and above, due to the high altitude. **Never underestimate the mountain**. It can be bitterly cold on the plateau, especially in rain or wind. A warm waterproof windcheater is essential, while a woolly balaclava or hat, warm pullover and gloves are advisable. It is also advisable to take dry clothes double-packed in plastic bags, and a pair of rubber sandals or thongs to change into at Panar Laban if your feet get soaked. On a fine day it is easy to get sunburnt in the thin air, particularly during the descent later in the day, so a hat and sun-block should also be taken. Other useful items are headache tablets, tissues and high energy food such as chocolates, raisins and nuts, or muesli bars.

Although there are water tanks along the trail all the way up to Panar Laban, there are none above Sayat-Sayat and a water bottle is advisable for this last stretch. Some people find that stopping every hour or so on the ascent with a small snack and a hot drink (take a thermos) or packet drink like Milo, reduces the onset of altitude effects. Cameras and film should be placed in plastic bags.

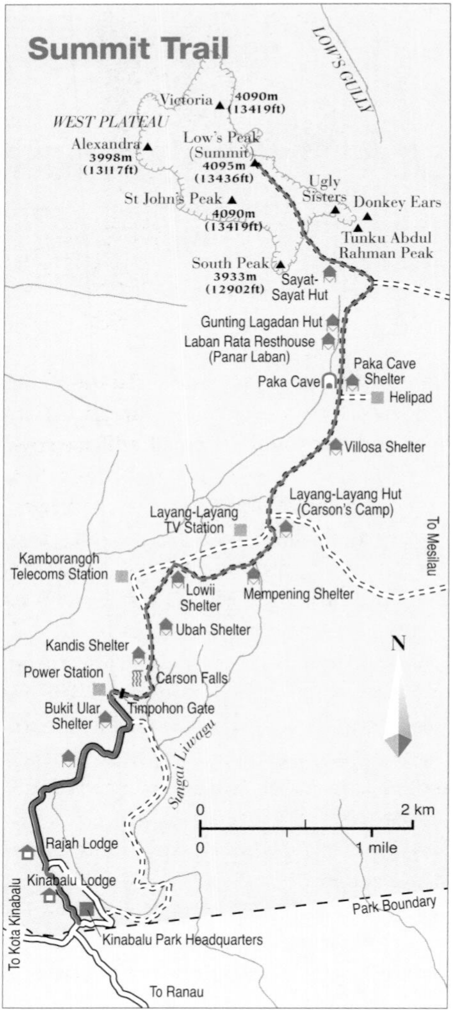

Surprisingly, the short first section of the rough gravel and sand track leads down, not up, across a small gully to join the main flank of the mountain, and past the little trickle of Carson's falls, named after the first Park Warden. From here the trail rises steadily as a series of rough, uneven steps, right up to the overnight huts at Panar Laban at 3,272 metres (10,735 feet).

*Mountain Blackbird*

There are no toilets along the trail, but small shelters, known as *pondoks*, named after common or interesting plants in the area, afford the weary some well earned rest at intervals and water tanks are provided at these shelters so climbers do not have to carry heavy water bottles with them. As it often rains on Kinabalu in the afternoons it is advisable to start as early as possible to avoid any downpour. The average time taken to reach Panar Laban is about four or five hours. Photographers, botanists and birdwatchers should expect to take rather longer.

The first trail shelter, Pondok Kandis, is reached at 1,981 metres (6,499 feet), where excellent views are to be had looking down to the coast. The orange bell-shaped flowers of *Rhododendron stenophyllum,* arranged in ones and twos with its small, stiff, narrow leaves, occur on the trail lower down. But particularly common here is the orange-flowered *R.fallacinum*, the shoots and undersides of its much broader leaves blanketed with a thick coat of coppery-gold scales. Even the compact heads of flowers are scattered with scales near the base.

A little further up, where the trail crests an exposed ridge, the first starry-flowered bushes of *Leptospermum flavescens* can be seen, a species that is also common on degraded white sandy soils in the lowlands. Moist winds blow refreshingly up the valley here and the gnarled trees leaning out from the ridge top are draped in trailing club mosses (*Lycopodium casuarinoides*) and pale green-grey

## Permits, guides and porters

A **permit** is required to climb the Mountain. At the time of writing this costs a maximum RM 50 per person (reductions for Malaysians and young people).

A **guide** is compulsory. The price for guiding is per group and ranges from RM30 to RM35 per day depending on the size of the group. These fees increase slightly if you choose to start and finish your climb at different places (Timpohan to Mesilau or vice versa).

**Porters** are available from around RM30 per day.

## Giant leech

Above Pondok Mempening where the trail runs over a rocky outcrop the rare giant Kinabalu leech has been seen, but only in pouring rain. This leech (which has still not been positively named) is bright orange-red and up to 30 centimetres (12 inches) or so in length. Almost nothing is known about it and its habits, but it is not a blood-sucker. It appears to feed mainly on the giant grey-blue Kinabalu earth-worms and to live in damp earth and leaves in cracks between the rocks.

lichens. The pink flowered *Rhododendron rugosum* with its rough bubble leaves is now quite common as a trail-side bush. The second shelter, Pondok Ubah at 2,081 metres (6,827 feet), is just below a well known site for what what must be one of Borneo's most unusual pitcher plants, *Nepenthes lowii*, but as it is slightly off the trail, ask your guide to point it out it to you.

Soon after, an overgrown track leads off left to the radio station, but the main trail continues to the right contouring around the ridge. The forest becomes thicker and more mossy, treeferns are abundant and everywhere the long spiky shoots of climbing bamboos pierce the mist. Another overgrown track here on the left leads steeply up to the TV station at Layang-Layang, but the main trail again continues on the right and out of the mossy forest of mixed bamboos and tree ferns. Several more rhododendrons start to occur and the beautiful golden yellow blooms of *Rhododendron retivenium* reach their upper limit here. *R. retivenium*, with its narrow leaves, should not be confused with the much larger *R.lowii* that starts here but becomes more common higher up. *R. lowii* is distinguished both by the fat broad leaves and the pinky yellow, rather than golden flowers. It often grows as a small tree rather than a shrub. At 2,515 metres (8,251 feet) the fourth shelter, Pondok Mempening, is reached, with wild begonias growing nearby. Stops at these shelters give one time to observe the squirrels, tree-shrews and birds that seem so unafraid and come looking for discarded food on the ground.

Soon one emerges onto an open exposed ridge at Layang-Layang, (previously known as Carson's Camp) at 2,702 metres (8,865 feet), where a small tin hut provides a welcome resting place (though not an overnight stop) for weary climbers.

At this point a band of ultramafic soil, distinguished by its orange-cinnamon colour, crosses the trail and the vegetation changes dramatically. The forest becomes shorter and much more open and is dominated by the second species of *Leptospermum* that grows on Kinabalu, *L. recurvum*, with its tiny grey leaves, and *Dacrydium gibbsiae*, a very beautiful conifer, both found only within the Kinabalu park. This is also the zone of the insect-eating pitcher plants for which Kinabalu is famous.

Out of the roughly 30 species of pitcher plants recorded from Borneo, around ten grow on the mountain and at least three are found nowhere else. These include the spectacular *Nepenthes rajah*, the largest pitcher plant in the world, and the bizarre but beautiful *N.villosa*, the mouths of its pinky-orange coloured pitchers ringed with a flamboyant necklace of sharp plates. This patch of ultramafic forest on the Summit Trail is the only place in the world that you are likely to see *N.villosa* growing in the wild, but the pitchers, nestling at the base of the *Leptospermum* trees in the moss, are easily damaged by trampling feet. Please look carefully where you tread. Another beautiful pitcher plant found in a few places just off the trail is *Nepenthes x kinabaluensis*, a hybrid between *N.villosa* and *N.rajah*, that has bigger pitchers than *villosa* but with a very reduced necklace of plates around the mouth. Ask your guide where you can see it.

At about 2,690 metres (8,825 feet), Pondok Villosa is situated at the top of an open rocky patch and soon the forest becomes even more stunted. Among the grey of the *Leptospermum* and the green of the *Dacrydium*, the scurfy orange young leaves of the endemic Haviland's oak (*Lithocarpus havilandii*) add a touch of colour. Superb vistas can be had of the mountain towering above as you follow the path upwards. An unusual conifer that occurs at Park HQ but becomes very common here is the Celery Pine (*Phyllocladus hypophyllus*). The tough diamond-shaped 'leaves' are in fact only flattened stems or *phyllodes*, the true leaves having been reduced to tiny scales at the 'leaf' edge.

The bubbly-leaved *Rhododendron rugosum* is now common together with the tiny little red-flowered Heath Rhododendron, *R. ericoides*, another of Kinabalu's many endemics, which first makes its appearance here. A relative of the tea plant with beautiful large camellia-like flowers that is also common from here all the way up to Panar Laban and above is *Schima brevifolia*, whose young purple leaf flushes are just as beautiful as its striking white flowers.

At the top of this open area at about 3,050 metres (10,000 feet), a small track leads off to a helipad on the right and it is worth making this five minute side trip for the dramatic view of the towering peaks from the helipad on a clear day.

Shortly after the helipad junction, you suddenly leave the ultramafic soils. The forest again changes back to taller trees draped thickly in mosses, and orchids cover the ground in between tumbled granite boulders. It has been estimated that orchids can provide as much as 60% of the ground cover at this elevation, with the rather coarse leaved purple-and-white flowered *Eria grandis* dominant.

Within a few minutes you arrive at the sixth shelter, Pondok Paka at 3,080 metres (10,105 feet), named after the Paka Cave nearby, famous as the place where Low, Whitehead and others slept before making the final assault on the summit. The Paka Cave, on the edge of a small stream, is really nothing more than a large overhanging rock. It can be reached along a rather overgrown track to the left, which continues above the cave to join the main trail higher up. This detour is fairly steep but takes only a lit-

## Leaf colours

Visitors often notice the abundance of plants with bright red leaf flushes. This is particularly common in plants higher up the mountain, and is thought to protect young leaves from damage by strong sunlight, as well as from attacks by leaf eaters by masking the green chlorophyll with unpalatable red and purple anthocyanins. In plants such as the mountain bilberries (*Vaccinium* spp), these colours are often more attractive and showy than the flowers. Other plants have a covering of coppery scales, or a silver-grey bloom which perform the same function.

tle longer than the standard route. For those particularly interested in plants or birds it can be worthwhile, and is now probably one of the best places in the park to see the Kinabalu Friendly Warbler or the elusive Blue Shortwing.

Large numbers of earthworm casts are often seen in this area together with digging marks made by one of the mountain's few high elevation creatures – the Kinabalu Ferret-badger. Like the leech, little is known about the ferret-badger but it is thought to be quite common at this altitude, feeding mainly on large, grey earthworms. Mountain Tree-shrews are more easily seen, often foraging through crumbs dropped by climbers.

The thinning air makes it harder to breathe, but the accommodation complex of Panar Laban (3,270 metres/10,728 feet) that can sleep 140 persons a night lies not far ahead. The most comfortable place to stay overnight is the Laban Rata resthouse which can hold 60 people and which is equipped with running water, electricity, a restaurant, and indoor showers and toilets (for details see **Planning and Practicalities**, page 25). Electric heaters are provided in the rooms as well as blankets. Some climbers opt to stay at Sayat-Sayat hut 400 metres (1,300 feet) higher to shorten the summit day. The facilities are much more basic here, with no heaters and an outside toilet several metres away. Food and sleeping bags have to be carried up and it is much colder.

If staying at Panar Laban the next phase of the climb begins at about 0300am the next day when you are woken for an early breakfast (at least a hot drink is advisable) and the climb up to Sayat-Sayat and the summit plateau. Above Panar Laban the trail continues as a series of wooden ladders, fashioned out of tree roots and branches, and a good torch is essential. This gives way to flatter, more easy walking just below Sayat-Sayat, when the true edge of the tree-line is reached. Ropes are fixed at difficult places, but these are more to inspire confidence than from necessity. Tough grasses and other plants cling to rock crevices, flowering and fruiting when only a few centimetres tall. From here the bare granite slabs stretch endlessly ahead to the pile of jumbled rocks that is Low's Peak – reached at last in time to catch the sunrise.

Above Sayat-Sayat, a series of small cairns linked by guide ropes lead to the summit. If the clouds come down during the descent, it is essential that climbers stay close to these ropes to avoid getting lost.

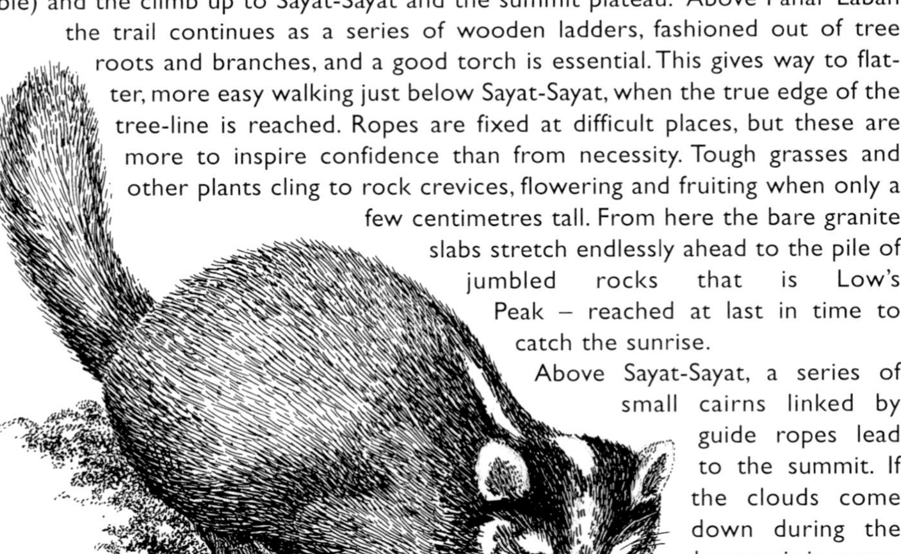

*Kinabalu Ferret-badger*

# CLIMBING ROUTES

The summit plateau of the mountain is divided by the chasm of Low's Gully, more than 1km (300 feet) deep, into two arms: the eastern and western plateaux. Though the standard Summit Trail to Low's Peak on the western plateau needs no climbing experience, other peaks are not so straightforward and mostly require ropes, though they are not necessarily difficult in climbing terms. Written permission from the Park authorities is required for any exploration away from the standard trail.

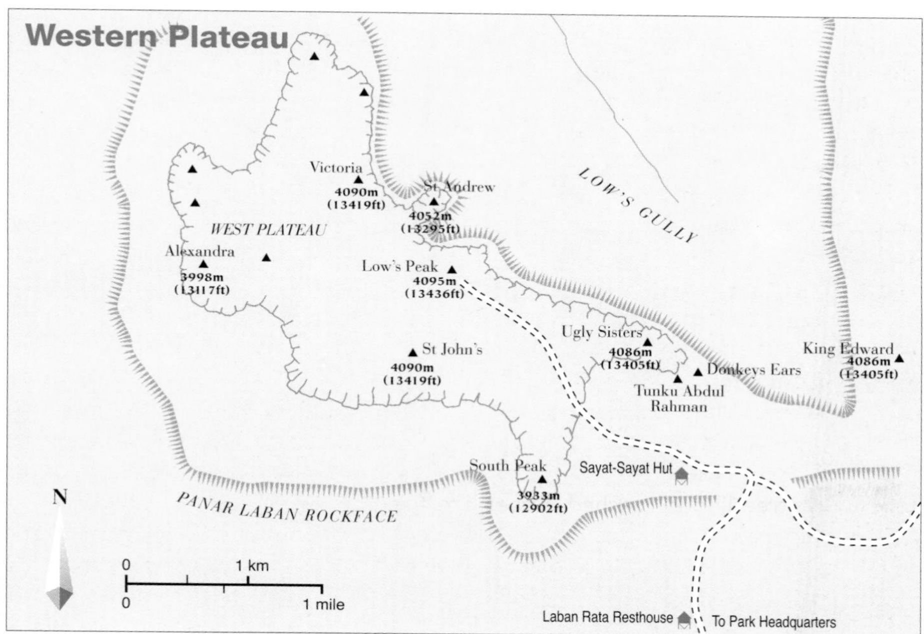


## WESTERN SUMMIT PLATEAU

On the western plateau (see map above) there are several peaks such as St John's (4,090 metres/13,419 feet) and South Peak (3,921 metres/12,864 feet), that can be climbed in a morning, though those who have little experience should be accompanied by experienced climbers and should use ropes wherever suitable. St John's in particular should not be attempted without ropes. More details about these routes can be found in the Sabah Society publication, *Kinabalu – Summit of Borneo*, published in 1996.

The small shelter on the western summit plateau known as the West Gurkha Hut, situated about 20 minutes walk beyond Low's Peak at an elevation of about 3,839 metres (12,595 feet) is available for small parties of experienced climbers who wish to spend more time exploring the western plateau, but climbers must bring all their equipment with them.

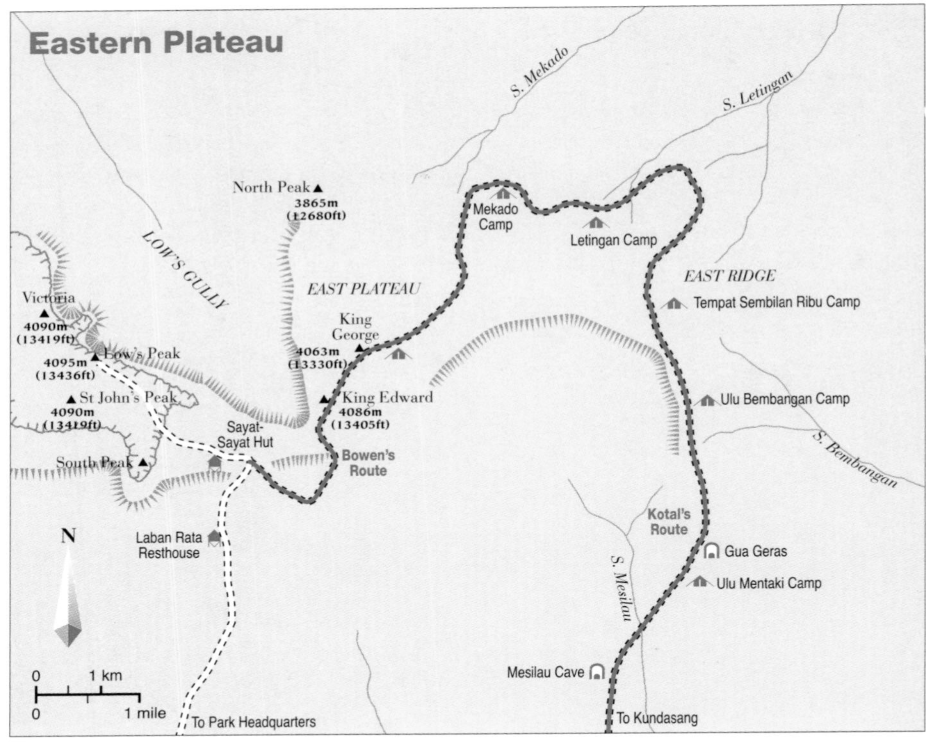


## EASTERN PLATEAU (BOWEN'S ROUTE)

The eastern plateau is about the same area as the western plateau but has a more rugged appearance, with more loose rock. Much more difficult to reach than the western plateau, the first recorded climb was not until 1956 when Myles Bowen and Harry Morris, employees of the oil company Shell, pioneered what is now known as Bowen's route which starts as a rough track leading off to the right above Panar Laban. The entrance is not marked. The track initially leads down more than 300 metres (around 1,000 feet) to skirt a steep rock slab, then through scrubby *Leptospermum* and *Rhododendron* forest and through a rock gully to a projecting spur with lovely views, before rising slightly over some small rocky ledges to the rock cliffs at the base of the eastern plateau. From here it is rock climbing all the way, including a seven metre (23 foot) chimney. Aluminium ladders and ropes have been fixed over the most difficult parts of the climb, but this is still a dramatic and memorable route and challenging for the non-climber. Permission must be obtained from the Park authorities before attempting this route and all climbers must be accompanied by an experienced mountain guide.

Once up onto the plateau itself the terrain is less steep but still rougher than the ice-smoothed slopes of the western plateau, with King Edward Peak (4,086 metres/13,405 feet) to the left and Mesilau Peak (3,801 metres/12,470 feet) to the

RIGHT: MAPS AND SIGNS GUIDE VISITORS AROUND A WIDE NETWORK OF PARK TRAILS.

BELOW LEFT: THE EXTRAORDINARY STARBURST FUNGI IS ONE OF MANY UNUSUAL SPECIES FOUND IN THE PARK. IT FLOURISHES ON THE LITTER AND EXPOSED ROOTS OF THE FOREST FLOOR.

BELOW RIGHT: LOOKING ALMOST PRIMAEVAL, THE TRILOBITE BEETLE FEEDS IN PATCHES OF MOSS ON ROTTING LOGS.

LEFT: NOISY AND CONSPICUOUS, GREEN MAGPIES CAN SOMETIMES BE SEEN ALONG THE ROAD AROUND THE PARK HEADQUARTERS.

BELOW: BARKING DEER ARE SHY DENIZENS OF THE LOWLAND FORESTS, OCCASIONALLY GLIMPSED WHEN THEY EMERGE AT THE FOREST EDGE TO FEED.

RIGHT: THE BEAUTIFUL BUT SHY WHITEHEAD'S TROGON FREQUENTS THE MIDDLE STORY OF MORE UNDISTURBED FOREST ALONG THE QUIETER TRAILS.

BELOW: YELLOW-THROATED MARTENS HAVE BEEN OBSERVED COMING DOWN TO DRINK ALONG SOME OF THE STREAMSIDE TRAILS NEAR PARK HEADQUARTERS.

ABOVE: MANY SPECIES OF GINGERS THRIVE ON THE LOWLAND FOREST FLOOR.

ABOVE: THE TINY, THIMBLE-FLOWERED HEATH RHODODENDRON IS ENDEMIC TO KINABALU.

ABOVE: RHODODENDRON BROOKEANUM IS ONE OF KINABALU'S MOST SPECTACULAR FLOWERS, OFTEN SEEN IN FULL BLOOM AROUND THE PARK HEADQUARTERS.

right. King Edward is the highest point on the eastern plateau but is dangerous even for experienced climbers. The most accessible peak here, which requires nothing more than a long, hard slog, is King George (4,062 metres/13,330 feet) which gives sweeping views across Low's Gully to Low's Peak and the other peaks of the western plateau as well as of the north ridge sloping down into thick montane forest towards Gunung Tamboyukon and of the eastern ridge leading down to Poring. A registration book is kept under a rock on King George Peak which climbers are requested to sign.

## EASTERN PLATEAU VIA EASTERN RIDGE (KOTAL'S ROUTE).

Another route to the the eastern plateau pioneered during the Royal Society Expeditions in 1964 takes from 4-7 days, depending on how large and fit the group is and how fast it is able to travel. This route is sometimes called Kotal's route after the guide who took the members of the Expedition to the eastern ridge – though hard and steep, it requires no real climbing ability.

This route starts from Kundasang, goes across the Pinosok plateau and past the Mesilau Cave, over the landslide with *Nepenthes rajah* on the other side of the Mesilau stream to the top of the hill, through ultramafic forest to the small Menteki river at about 1,800 metres (5,900 feet). The second day leads up a steep narrow ridge before a 20 minute steep descent to the head of the Bembangan river at about 2,750 metres (9,000 feet), to camp for the night. Very fit climbers can reach this campsite in one day. The next morning, after trekking back up to the ridge, the trail continues upwards to about 3,250 metres (10,700 feet). Here it opens out at the base of the Mesilau Pinnacles to superb views all around including the curiously shaped Rhino Horn which blocked the path of the Royal Society Expedition up the eastern ridge from Poring. It is not possible to climb the Pinnacles here and one must continue scrambling around their base, up and down, always steep, often using tree roots and branches to swing down vertical sections of rock or ropes to cross particularly tricky stretches. At the end of the third or fourth day at the Letingan stream campsite (3,050 metres/10,000 feet), you have gained no altitude but are about halfway round the base of the pinnacles. Excellent views looking north to Gunung Tamboyukon are had from this campsite. The next day the trail continues to wind around below the pinnacles, even in one place clambering down a steep waterfall, using ropes, to the Ulu Mekado campsite (3,100 metres/10,200 feet) where, at last, the route leads you to the head of the Mekado valley and up the steep sloping granite onto the eastern plateau.

## LOW'S GULLY

Low's Gully is without doubt the single most dramatic feature of the mountain from the climbing point of view, and was for a long time considered to be inaccessible. Reaching more than a kilometre (3,000 feet) down and more than 16 kilometres (10 miles) in length, the gully is shrouded with an air of mystery made only stronger by its inaccessibility. Several parties, including British army expeditions, have tried to penetrate the gully from either the top or the bottom – but all failed. More recently in

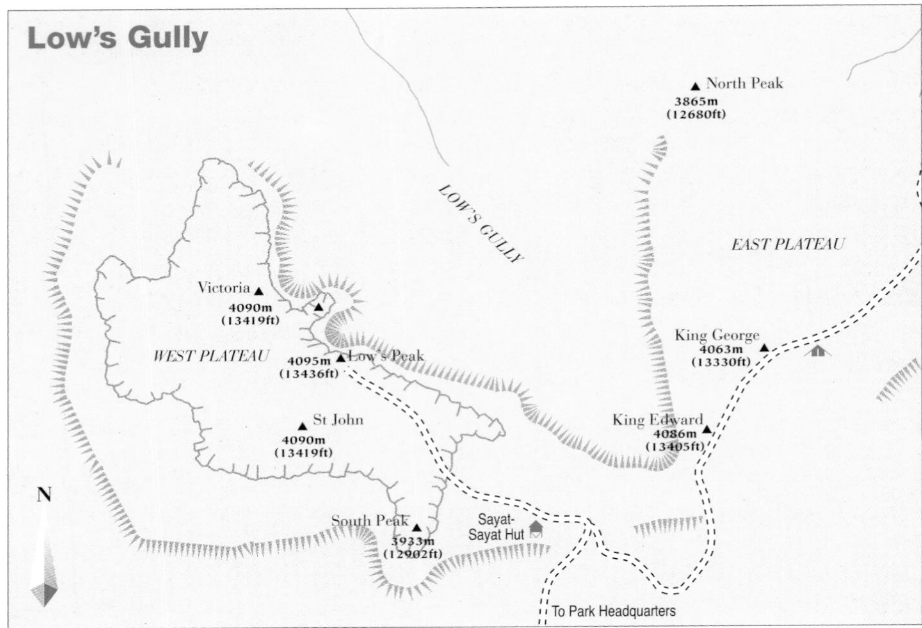


1998, however, a joint Malaysian–British mountaineering group made another, successful, attempt. Their success was, in a large part, due to the fact that the descent was made during the El Nino induced drought of 1998, and the climbers themselves said afterwards that in wet weather the descent would have been impossible. Indeed some members of the expedition felt that it was not so much a conquering of the gully, as an acceptance by the mountain to let them through, perhaps due to the spiritual rituals that took place both before and after the climb. The group also succeeded in descending, for the first time, the vertical cliffs at the head of the gully that come down from Commando Cauldron. Other proposals have been made to descend the gully since, but the Sabah Parks, wisely recognising the great dangers involved have not, so far, given permission for any further attempts. Low's Gully is included here only because it is such an obvious feature of the mountain and for its historical interest.

## Low's Gully

Though he never climbed Low's Peak, Sir Hugh Low was the first to look down into the dramatic gully that bears his name, saying "...looking down over the ridge, I gazed into a circular amphitheatre about 80 yards broad, the bottom of which from its great depth and my position overhanging it was undiscernible, though I imagine I could see down two thousand feet."

# Beyond the Mountain

Most visitors to Kinabalu arrive at Park HQ, and though some climb the mountain, for many the HQ is all they see of the park. Yet there is a wealth of other attractions to be found in the very different environments that lie in the lowlands around the mountain, and for the visitor with a little more time to spare, it is well worth making the efforts to visit these fascinating places.

Poring Hot Springs offers a canopy walkway through the tree tops, as well as relaxing sulphur pools and the possibility of seeing Rafflesia, monkeys and a host of lowland birdlife, while Mesilau is the only place in the park where you can see the giant insect-eating pitcher plant *Nepenthes rajah,* found nowhere else in the world.

Sayap too has much animal and plant life not found in any other accessible parts of the park, and an enjoyable trails system where you will rarely see another person. Serinsim in turn offers pleasant camping at the edge of the cool Kinarom River.

# KUNDASANG AND MESILAU

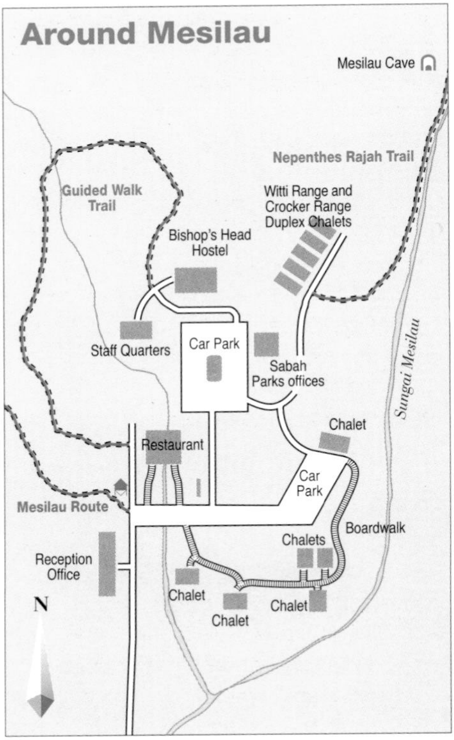

**AROUND THE MESILAU RESORT.** On the southern boundary of the Park, a few kilometres (miles) beyond the Park HQ, lies the Pinosok Plateau with an average elevation between 1,500-2,000 metres (5,000 – 6,500 feet). Once pristine forest, the plateau is a victim of one of the many boundary changes that the Park has suffered and is now dominated by vegetable farms and by the 18-hole Kinabalu golf course. But above the golf course lies the Mesilau Resort at 1,951 metres (6,380 feet), nestled at the very base of the mountain, under its towering pinnacles, on the banks of the swift-flowing East Mesilau river in almost untouched oak-chestnut forest and only just over two hours drive from Kota Kinabalu.

To reach the resort, follow the highway past the Park HQ, 6 kilometres (4 miles) down to Kundasang. Just beyond the vegetable stalls that are such a feature of Kundasang, the road turns left for another 11 kilometres (7 miles), descending steeply to cross the small Liwagu river. Kundasang is the centre of the highland vegetable industry in Sabah and rows of cabbages, tomatoes and onions terrace the hillsides. It is here, in the shadow of Kinabalu, that the garden memorial to allied soldiers who died during the second world war was erected.

Across the Liwagu river it is a steep haul up the other side, with one short rough unsealed patch for which a four wheel drive vehicle is sometimes needed. At the top a small road leads to a dairy farm on the left, where the odd cow may be seen grazing in the fields. On the right, just over the crest of the hill, black-netted low-roofed structures are mushroom houses where fresh Shitake mushrooms are produced. Another few minutes down, and over the West Mesilau river, takes you to a junction where the sealed road to the resort turns sharply left to reach the golf course. Here there is a complete change in scenery. The greens and fairways are lined with introduced pines and spectacular red-leaved Japanese Maples while yellow day-lilies, begonias and balsams provide bright splashes of colour. Here and there several remnant patches of the original forest have been left between the fairways. On a clear day there are superb views of the mountain from here with the jagged Mesilau Pinnacles running into the long precipitous eastern ridge that eventually leads down to Poring. Follow the signboards to the Mesilau Resort through the golf course to the Park boundary and into the montane forest, then along the frothing torrent of the East Mesilau river with superb views of the pinnacles above on a clear day.

Another road continues past the Golf Club and onto the main part of the Pinosok Plateau which, now cleared for vegetable farms, sweeps right up to the forest line of the park boundary. In fine weather, stop at the old KPD mulberry/silkworm farm on the roadside and walk up to the viewing shelter for magnificent panoramic views of the mountain.

## Mesilau programmes

An interpretation centre at the resort is run by the Sabah Parks staff. Guided trail walks lasting about half an hour are led every day – on weekdays at 09.30, 11.00 and 14.00; at weekends and on Public Holidays at 07.30, 10.30 and 14.00. There is no charge. As at Park HQ, school programmes and other special programmes can be arranged on written request to the Park HQ.

The resort can sleep 220 persons a night in secluded chalets or semi-detached lodges, as well as in more basic hostels (for details see **Planning and Practicalities**, page 25). The chalets are set individually amongst the trees on the banks of the East Mesilau river and sleep from 4 to 6 people each. When the resort was being built the policy was to disturb the natural forest as little as possible. Consequently even boardwalks connecting the chalets have been built around the trees and the luxuriant ground cover is largely undisturbed.

Heaters are provided in the chalets and lodges and electricity, from the resort's own generator, is currently provided 24 hours a day. The restaurant serves good western and local food though choices are somewhat limited. Self-catering facilities are available only in the individual chalets.

Wild rhododendrons, orchids and pitcher plants have been used in the landscaping to good effect. Other plants are abundant along the paths, such as the shrubby raspberry *Rubus fraxinifolius*, with its dry, sour fruit, together with a large coarse weedy plant in the daisy family (Compositae) with silvery hairy young leaves and a small round red-fruited plant in the potato family (Solanaceae). Avoid this as, surprisingly, many species in this family have poisonous fruits. A *Medinella* species with small leaves and small, pretty pink flower bunches is also common here in contrast to the large-leaved species that is most common at Park HQ and the mountain *Melastoma*, with it large pinkish flowers, hanging over the stream below the restaurant adds a touch of colour.

The resort is excellent for birdwatching, with a range of species very similar to that at Park HQ. Ashy Drongos and Bornean Treepies are equally common, while the dark brown Sunda Whistling Thrush is often seen lurking along the stream that runs under the restaurant or in the undergrowth by the chalets on the banks of the Mesilau river. It is impossible not to notice the flocks of Chestnut-capped Laughing-thrushes moving through the middle canopy in search of insects throughout the day. Mixed hunting parties of these Laughing-thrushes are often joined by Green Magpies, Black-and-Crimson Orioles and various flycatchers such as the Indigo Flycatcher (dark blue with a black face and pale crown) and the dark blue Snowy-browed Flycatcher (with its white eyebrow and rusty breast), as well as the striking black and white Little Pied Flycatcher. Especially memorable sights could be a pair of Grey-chinned Minivets playing in the tree-tops, their brilliant plumage (scarlet and black in the male, golden and black in the female) glowing in the sunshine, or the tiny but gorgeous Scarlet Sunbird darting about the rhododendron flowers. A characteristic sound of the mountain forest at this elevation is the rolling "took-took-terrook" call of the Golden-naped Barbet, more often heard than seen due to its habit of sitting motionless in the top of a tree when calling and of being absolutely silent when feeding in fruiting trees. Barbets are remarkable birds in that their call is "hummed", with closed bill and the throat bulging out at every note, rather than sung. Of the nine Borneo barbet species, eight have been recorded from the mountain, each species with a distinctive, characteristic call. All except one (the plain Brown Barbet of the lowlands, found in the forests around Poring) have mostly green plumage with a distinctive rainbow of colours adorning the head and neck. The Golden-naped Barbet, a Borneo endemic found only on the islands's higher mountains, and up to 3,000 metres (6,200 feet) on Kinabalu, is less gaudy than most, its head being pale blue with a golden collar.

Animal life at Mesilau is also similar to that at park HQ, with Jentinck's Squirrel, the Bornean Mountain Ground Squirrel and the Mountain Tree-shrew all common. If you are lucky you may even see one speciality that is hardly ever seen at the Park HQ, a group of lovely Maroon Langurs with thick russet fur, almost like teddy-bears, which visits the resort for a few days every now and then.

### Guided Walk Trail

The Guided Walk Trail (which can be done without a guide if you wish) starts near the Bishop's Head hostel, leading into the oak-chestnut forest, and takes about half an hour. The forest here is in a sheltered valley as compared to the ridge on which the Park HQ is situated and the trees are taller and more mossy. Acorns and chestnuts of several species usually lie along the path, often chewed by small animals.

The ground cover is thick with wild gingers, though their flowers are often inconspicuous and close to the ground, and mosses and epiphytes are abundant. The long-leaved Bird's Nest Fern is particularly noticeable as an epiphyte in the trees. Near the top of a small rise some particularly large *Dacrydium* conifers can be seen with tall thick trunks and feathery foliage against the sky. Down the other side the path crosses the same little stream that flows under the restaurant and down to meet the Mesilau river. On the other side of this little stream the trees are thickly clad in mosses and liverworts with long trails hanging down almost like tattered curtains or leafy green tinsel. Just by the stream itself, some unusually large plants of the mountain ginger *Alpinia havilandii* occur and the pink-flowered Kinabalu Balsam grows on the rocky banks.

Many of the ginger flowers in the montane forest are pollinated by small bees and the recently discovered Mountain Honey-bee (*Apis nuluensis*) appears to be specially common at Mesilau. This bee builds its combs in holes in trees and the nests are raided by the local people for their honey wherever they are found, but it was not until 1996 that the species was described. Its discovery raised the number of *Apis* honey-bees in Borneo to five out of the eight known, more than anywhere else in the world. Perhaps this is why tales of Honey Bears frequenting the area were so common in the past. Major initiatives on tropical honey-bee research, including *Apis nuluensis*, are now being undertaken by the government agricultural research station at Lagud Sebrang, Tenom, in Sabah.

Soon the forest becomes more open and the delicate climbing bamboo (*Bambusa gibbsiae*) drapes the trees in its turn. Glimpses of the restaurant can be caught across the valley here, before the path re-enters the taller oak-chestnut forest to come out just outside the restaurant complex.

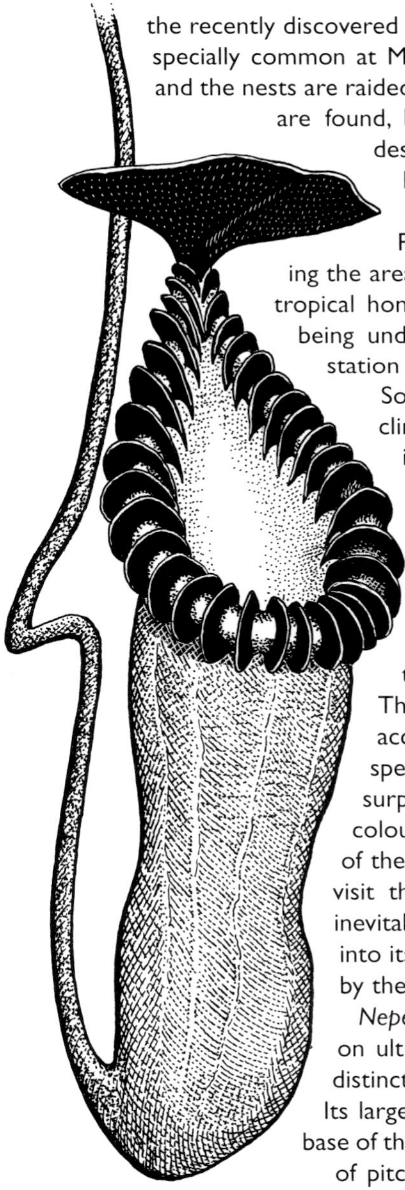

### *Nepenthes rajah* Trail

(Ten minutes to the West Mesilau river, another ten minutes to the top of the trail)

The Mesilau area is well-known as one of the few accessible localities in the Kinabalu Park in which the spectacular pitcher plant *Nepenthes rajah* grows. It may surprise some people to learn that the bizarre, often colourful cup of the pitcher plant is not a flower, but part of the leaf – a trapping device to obtain nutrients. Insects visit the pitchers to collect nectar and some of these inevitably fall into the liquid-filled cup and drown, dissolving into its enzyme-rich fluid. The nutrients are then absorbed by the plant through the walls of the pitcher.

*Nepenthes rajah*, another of Low's discoveries, grows only on ultramafic soils within the Kinabalu Park and has the distinction of being the largest pitcher plant in the world. Its large magenta cups reclining on the ground around the base of the plant can hold up to two litres. While the usual diet of pitcher plants is insects, other creatures such as frogs and centipedes have been found occasionally, and in the case of *N.rajah*, even small rats. A pitcher may produce enzymes for as much as six months or more before it starts to wither and turn brown. Though no longer an active trap at this stage, the rainwater filled pitchers on the ground provide a welcome water source for other creatures in times of drought for another six months or so before they start to

*Pitcher plant*
(Nepenthes edwardsiana)

rot and disintegrate.

Because *Nepenthes rajah* is so rare and restricted in habitat and because there have been problems with illegal collecting in the past, the site is strictly out of bounds to visitors unless accompanied by a Park guide, and visitors are charged a small fee.

The trail starts near the Crocker Range lodge leading down past the historic Mesilau Cave. This, like most so-called 'caves' on Kinabalu, is nothing more than a large rock overhang, but in the early days it was a hunter's camp, and the only place to stay for visitors who wished to explore the *Nepenthes rajah* site and beyond. The trail continues down past the cave, and for about ten minutes along a low ridge above the stream with lots of large mossy rocks and boulders covered in ferns, liverworts and orchids. After about ten minutes, the frothing Mesilau river is reached. The river is crossed by a short suspension bridge before the trail goes steeply up the old landslide on the right on the opposite bank, covered in scrubby shrubs, grasses, orchids and rhododendrons. The whole landslide is on the ultramafic soils and many of the plants here are distinct and found only on these soils. Another ten minutes or so brings you up to the more overgrown top of the landslide, with small trees, where the vegetation is thicker and where the best pitchers are found. The occasional *Nepenthes lowii* as well as the dainty little *Nepenthes tentaculata* grow here as well. It is worth taking a look inside the *N.rajah* pitchers to see mosquito larvae, and sometimes the grub-like rat-tailed hover-fly larvae, swimming around. Frog eggs have also been seen laid in the upper part of pitchers of *N.tentaculata*.

When coming back down the trail, superb views can be had of the montane forest canopy along the river, the almost vertical rock slopes beyond the resort covered with sparse vegetation, and the spectacular stark rock ring of the Mesilau Pinnacles above, with cascading waterfalls in wet weather, which bar the direct route to the eastern plateau.

## Living inside pitchers

As well as their prey, pitcher plants are home to over 150 different species of animal at one point or another in their life-cycle, especially mosquitoes and flies which breed in the water filled cups. The larvae of some species which are unharmed by the enzymes colonise the pitchers at an early stage, while other pitchers are only colonised after they have turned brown and filled with rainwater.

Some larvae are carrion feeders and share the pitcher's prey, others feed on detritus left from the dead insects, while others are filter-feeders, skimmimg off bacteria from the liquid. Yet others are carnivorous, feeding on the other inhabitants of the cup. Spiders, crabs and ants have all been recorded living in mutual benefit with lowland species of pitcher plants and even frog eggs and tadpoles have been found in the water filled cups. Fewer such associations have been found in the mountain species on Kinabalu, which are far less studied.

KINABALU'S UNUSUAL ULTRAMAFIC FOREST AT AROUND AROUND 2500 METRES (8000 FEET) ON THE SUMMIT TRAIL CONTAINS SEVERAL RARE AND ENDEMIC SPECIES OF FLORA AND FAUNA.

LEFT: CLIMBERS USE FIXED ROPES TO ASCEND THE PRECIPITOUS SLOPES OF THE EASTERN RIDGE.

BELOW LEFT: THE INDIGO FLY-CATCHER HAWKS INSECTS IN THE FOREST UNDERSTOREY AND IS OFTEN SEEN PERCHED ON THE STREET LAMPS AT THE PARK HEAD-QUARTERS

BELOW RIGHT: MOUNTAIN TREESHREWS FORAGE MAINLY ON THE GROUND.

OPPOSITE RIGHT: THE KINABALU FERRET-BADGER IS FOUND AT HIGH ALTITUDES ON THE SUMMIT TRAIL.

OPPOSITE BELOW: SEVERAL SPECIES OF PITCHER PLANT ARE FOUND ON KINABALU, INCLUDING *NEPENTHES KINABALUENSIS* (LEFT) AND *NEPENTHES LOWII* (RIGHT). THE FORMER OCCURS NOWHERE ELSE IN THE WORLD.

ABOVE: THE DISTINCTIVE 'DONKEY'S EARS' PEAKS MARK KINABALU'S SUMMIT PLATEAU.

ABOVE: FORESTS OF TREEFERNS THRIVE IN THE SHELTERED GULLIES ALONG THE SUMMIT TRAIL.

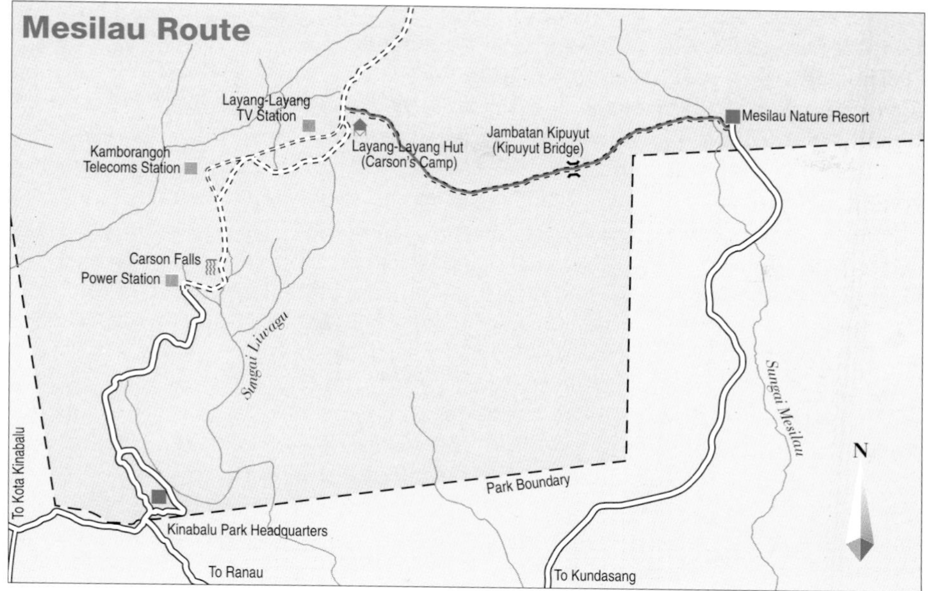


## MESILAU ROUTE

The Mesilau Route leading from the resort to Layang-Layang (Carson's Camp) at 2,702 metres (8,865 feet) on the Summit Trail was opened only in October 1998. This route is used mainly by scientists and researchers as it takes longer (about 5-6 hrs to Layang-Layang from Mesilau, as compared to 2-3 hrs on the standard route to Timpohon Gate), and many parts are steep and slippery, particularly in wet weather. Visitors who wish to use this trail must register and pay a small fee either at the Timpohon Gate at the base of the Summit Trail or at the Mesilau Gate at the other end before they start.

The start of the trail from the Mesilau Gate up to the first steep descent is an enjoyable walk in itself that only takes about one hour, one way. The trail starts from a small shelter just above the reception office in the tall oak-chestnut forest, but conifers soon become more common and climbing bamboos dominate the undergrowth. Some superb *Agathis* trees grow here and those near the path that have been damaged in the past can be seen oozing a thick white resin or *dammar*. In olden days this *dammar* was much sought after as fuel for lighting fires and lamps and trees were tapped regularly. Indeed *Agathis dammar* was one of Borneo's main forest produce exports in the past. After about 20 minutes, near the ridge crest at about 2,000 metres (6,500 feet), the forest suddenly becomes much shorter and more stunted, with rocks and boulders jumbled among tangled tree roots, covered in spongy mosses and liverworts. On the boulders and lower trunks and branch-es are many delicate orchids and on the top of the ridge small-leaved *Leptospermum* trees, conifers, and other trees and shrubs typical of the exposed mossy ridges become dominant, in particular the beautiful orange-flowered *Rhododendron fallacinum* with its coppery-scaled leaves.

The path soon rises steeply once again to an open patch dominated by *Dipteris* ferns, before levelling off slightly, still following the narrowing ridge crest which opens out at the top (2,286 metres/7,475 feet), giving stunning views of the mountain above, if it is clear, and of the waterfalls and rock faces above the resort, as well as views over to the Trus Madi range to the south-east. The vegetation here becomes much more open and stunted, dominated by *Leptospermum* and *Dacrydium*.

The ridge-top is reached just before the 1½ km mark. Here the trail starts to descend quite steeply down the other side, through taller forest with climbing bamboos. Some little streams are crossed before reaching the Kipuyut bridge, a suspension bridge across the swift-flowing West Mesilau river at 2,073 metres (6,778 feet), that cascades down from the precipitous slopes of the Eastern plateau above. The bridge gets its name from the large trees in the area here that provided shelter in heavy rain for local people in the past. A little further on, near the 3km mark, a smaller tributary of the West Mesilau is crossed. From here the trail follows the ridge, rising steeply and continuously, up and up and up in an almost never-ending series of steps for about 2½ kms (1½ miles), with occasional views across to the Summit Trail as you get higher. At last you reach a very narrow col which joins onto the main Kinabalu massif. From here another 500 metres (¼ mile) of trail, more or less contouring around the massif, will bring you out onto the Summit Trail, a little way above Layang-Layang (Carson's Camp). The whole route from Mesilau to Layang-Layang is 5.7 km (3½ miles).

This route has been advertised in the past as an alternative route to the first part of the summit climb, but it is very much longer and more arduous than the standard trail which is only about 3 km (2 miles) from Timpohon Gate to Layang-Layang. It is recommended that the Mesilau Route is walked separately.

The trail is a good one for people who are more interested in the plants and wildlife than in the actual summit climb as it is much less frequented and consequently the wildlife is less disturbed than on the Summit Trail. The easiest way to walk it would be from the Summit Trail end, arranging at Park HQ for transport to collect you from the Mesilau resort before you start. For those who don't wish to walk the whole trail, the path from the Mesilau Gate up to the top of the ridge, down to the Kipuyut Bridge and back is a pleasant 2½ – 3 hour walk for the reasonably fit.

# PORING HOT SPRINGS

## THE ROAD TO PORING.

The Poring Hot Springs ranger station lying 40 kilometres (25 miles) from Park HQ in the humid lowlands is a complete contrast to the cool environment of Park HQ. The sealed road to Poring leads past the cabbage and flower farms of Kundasang and beyond, to the town of Ranau and the lowlands. From the road just beyond Kundasang, magnificent vistas can be had on a clear day of the mountain's eastern summit and long eastern ridge. The bare scar of the recently closed Mamut Copper Mine can be seen on the eastern flank of the mountain and once past Ranau the mine's huge sludge pond becomes visible in the distance.

The road leads past the sludge pond before turning in towards the mountain again and to Poring itself, which can be recognised by the ever increasing number of local gift stalls that have been set up just outside the entrance gate. A speciality here is the variety of beautiful rock souvenirs ranging from jade-green malachite and golden pyrites through purply-gold irridescent peacock-ore to stark black and white granite.

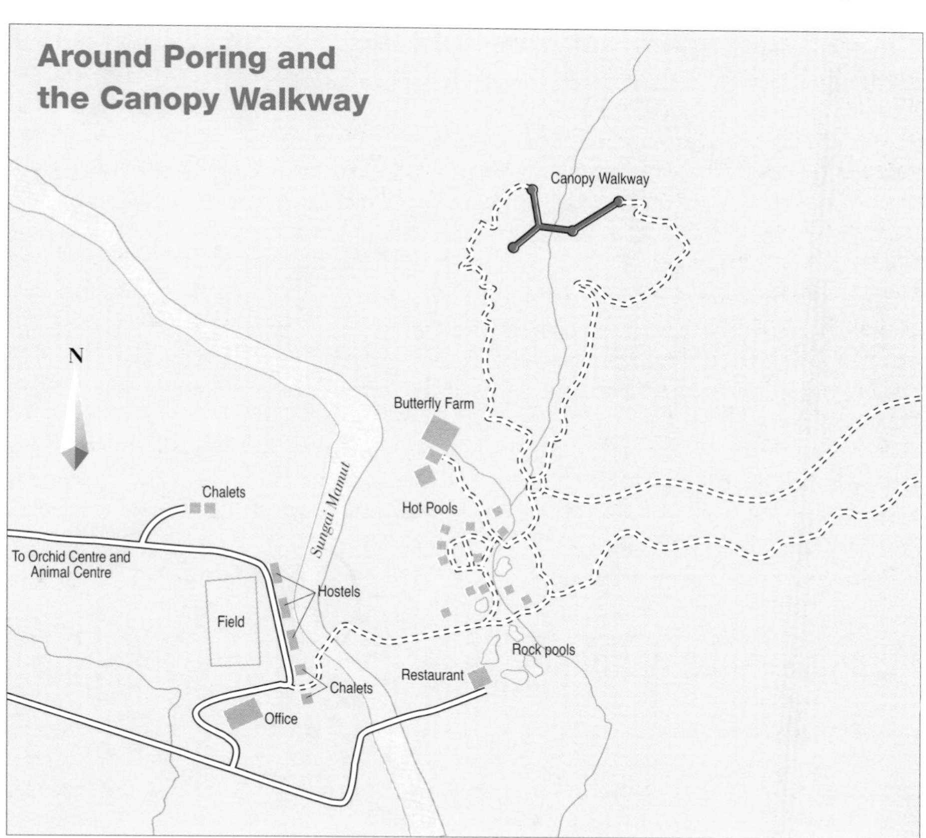

## PORING HEADQUARTERS

The headquarters of the Poring Hot Springs ranger station, at an elevation of 550 metres (1,800 feet), lies on the Park boundary at the edge of the Mamut river. Offices, visitor chalets and hostels are situated here as well as the Orchid Conservation centre and the fenced 5 acre tropical garden nearby containing an animal rehabilitation centre. The main attractions here, however, are the hot and cold pools in a forest clearing on the other side of the Mamut river. Other attractions across the river are a small butterfly enclosure, a forest trail system, a Canopy walkway and picnic areas. Night walks on the canopy walkway can be arranged on request and school and other special programmes can be arranged if a written request is made in advance.

**Mamut copper mine**

The Mamut Copper Mine was started in 1975, when about 25 square kilometres (10 square miles) of the Park were excised to allow for its development. The huge open-cast mine produced 400 tons of copper ore concentrate a day as well as small quantities of gold and silver but was closed at the end of 1999. In total, 580,000 tonnes of copper, 43.5 tonnes of gold, and 284 tonnes of silver were mined. Presently the area is proposed for development as a mountain resort over a 20 year period.

The chalets and hostels can accommodate 90 persons per night and all have self-catering facilities (see **Planning and Practicalities** page 25). There are also stalls serving local food just outside the entrance gate, and a restaurant at the hot pools clearing, serving both western and oriental food. It is advisable to take a torch if eating at the restaurant in the evening as well as raincoats and umbrellas in wet weather.

Most people who visit Poring come just for the day – over 150,000 a year, to enjoy the hot waters. By evening they are gone, leaving the clearing to the frogs and the bats. All visitors are required to pay a fee for coming into the Park. Fees are also payable for entrance to the Canopy walkway, the butterfly farm, the orchid centre and the animal centre.

### Orchids and Rafflesia

Orchids and Rafflesia are, perhaps, the two groups of plants that are associated with Kinabalu more than any others.

The superb lowland orchid conservation centre here was started in 1987, covering about four hectares (10 acres), with beautifully landscaped orchid houses and plant displays. Plants from all over Sabah are included, though the majority are from Kinabalu and its surroundings.

The Poring orchid centre was originally set up as a sister centre to the one in Tenom in southern Sabah, run by the Agriculture Department. The rationale was to spread the species and thus the risk in case of floods at the Tenom centre. More than 500 species are now grown at the Poring centre, many of them rare and endangered. Many other plants are also included in the collection with special emphasis being given to groups with horticultural potential such as palms, aroids, begonias and gingers.

The Sabah Parks have now built a micro-propagation laboratory at Poring and are looking into the possibility of ex-situ conservation of particularly rare species of both orchids and pitcher plants by micro-propagation. This could be particularly beneficial for groups such as the slipper orchids, which are of high horticultural value. Six out of the twelve Borneo slipper orchids are found on the mountain, including the recently discovered *Paphiopedilum kolopakingii*, previously known only from Kalimantan, and the rare Rothschild's slipper orchid (*P. rothschildianum*) with its striped outstretched petals reaching as much as 30 centimetres (12 inches) across. Rothschild's Slipper orchid is known from only a few protected localities within the Kinabalu Park but is cultivated at both the Mountain Garden at Park HQ and at the Orchid Centre at Poring. In the wild Slipper orchids tend to flower only once a year in March or April, but those in cultivation sometimes flower at other times. The main flowering season for most orchids at Poring is October to February, as at Park HQ.

Orchids at the Poring centre also include several species of the horticulturally important *Dendrobium* and *Bulbophyllum* orchids, many with large showy flowers. *Bulbophyllum*, with over 90 species on the mountain, is the largest genus of orchids in Borneo and boasts flowers ranging from the size of a fingernail to the spectacular *B.virescens* with inflorescences more than 30 centimetres (12 inches) across.

Another interesting species is the yellow-flowered *Vanilla kinabaluensis*, a magnificent climbing orchid that casts huge trails of succulent green leaves and stems over giant forest trees. It is related to *Vanilla planifolia* from Central America that produces the vanilla spice of commerce, but though the Borneo species have beautiful bunches of creamy-green flowers, they do not have any commercial value as a spice.

Other orchids with attractive flowers are the rat-tailed orchids (*Paraphalaenopsis*) with slender leaves almost as much as a metre (a yard) long, the gorgeous scarlet-flowered spider orchid *Renanthera bella,* and the species of *Phalaenopsis*. *P. gigantea*, the Elephant's Ear orchid, boasts the largest leaves of any orchid in the world, while the Moth or Moon orchid, (*P. amabilis*), with snowy-white flowers held on long arching sprays is probably the most popular orchid in Sabah, seen growing in old coconut husks under house eaves in almost every *kampung* that you pass.

All these are epiphytes, trailing their blooms across the path or dangling from a tree branch over a stream. Common ground orchids include the striking *Phaius tankervilleae* that has been planted all around the Poring HQ complex and the white-flowered *Calanthe triplicata* often seen along the forest trails.

The spectacular Rafflesia grows wild in

**Activities at Poring**

Poring has a range of activities for the visitor to enjoy. These include:

- Butterfly Centre
- Night Walks
- Schools and educational programmes
- Orchid Centre
- Tropical Garden
- Forest trails
- Canopy walkway
- Animal rehabilitation centre

these forests as well. A parasite, Rafflesia has no stem or leaves of its own and gets its nourishment from thread-like filaments spreading through the roots and stem of its host forest vines. The buds appear as small knobs covered in dark brown bracts on the stem of the vine and take about nine months to develop to the size of a cabbage before they open. The flowers are notorious for their bad smell, but this has been exaggerated and in any case lasts no more than a few hours, to attract pollinators, while the bloom itself lasts three to four days. Two species have been found on Kinabalu, the huge *Rafflesia keithii*, which really is a giant, growing up to a whopping 94 centimetres (37 inches) across and the smaller *R.pricei*, about 30 centimetres (12 inches) across.

All efforts to bring Rafflesia into cultivation in the past have failed, or had uncertain results. Recently, however, the Sabah Parks carried out successful inoculations of the host vine in two different locations near Poring. After the specially treated seeds were planted, the results were awaited anxiously. At last, earlier this year, small brown buds were observed busting through the bark – a major scientific breakthrough for Sabah Parks.

Poring was once famous for the Rafflesia, but at present there are no known sites within the park. There are, however, several places outside the Park boundary where Rafflesia grows on private land and where visitors can see the huge flower for a small fee paid to the landowner, although the flowers are mainly the smaller *R. pricei*. This scheme (which was initiated by the Park staff in 1994), provides a welcome incentive to local landowners to preserve any Rafflesia growing on their land. The Park staff will know if there are flowers at any of these sites, but the devastating effects of the El Nino induced droughts have taken their toll and several sites appear to be inactive at the time of writing.

### Hot Pools and Butterflies

The hot pools are scattered across a small clearing in the forest, reached by a short suspension bridge crossing the murky waters of the Mamut river and a short path leading past remnant forest trees and clumps of huge bamboos on the river bank. It is from these bamboos that Poring takes its name – *poring* being the local word for this bamboo that goes by the scientific

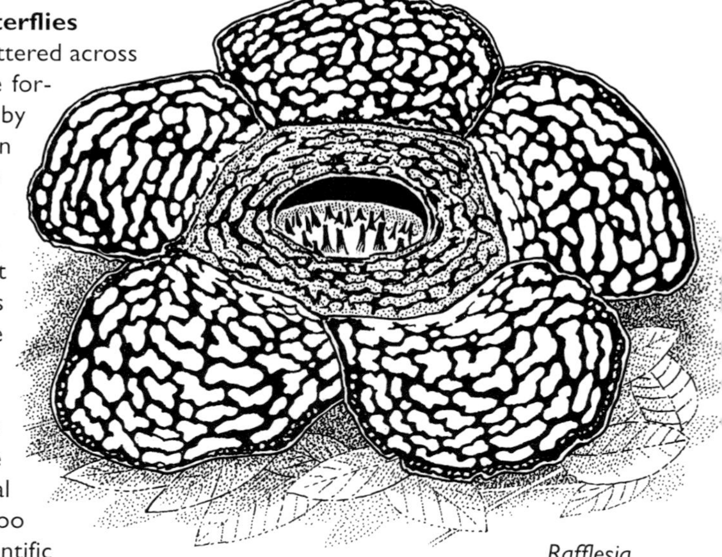

*Rafflesia*

name of *Gigantochloa levis*.

A long time ago, the very first site of Kampung Poring was higher up the mountain, just below a large grove of these bamboos. It was said that the bamboos growing there were especially large, wide enough to accommodate grown men, and that local hunters used them for shelter. During periods of tribal warfare, the village children would be hidden in the huge culms and collected only after any dispute had been settled. The bamboo groves were also said to serve as a sacred place for certain ritual practices. Today the bamboos are still used as a source of food, building materials and household utensils.

Just before the hot pools are reached a musky scent sometimes pervades the air. This comes from the seeds of the beautiful pink-flowered Cassia tree (*Cassia nodosa*), whose long dagger-like pods litter the ground in season. Large, papery white seeds, fallen here and and there on the path, are those of the Midnight Horror (*Oroxylum indicum*) named after the fleshy purple foul-smelling flowers that open at night to be pollinated by bats, and huge, rough hairy leaves together with small brown fruits covered in long, soft, blunt spines are from wild *tarap* trees (*Artocarpus odoratissimus*). Clumps of a large-leaved species of *Donax* with inconspicuous yellow flowers and leaves, often dotted with insect damage, line the path. Scattered throughout the clearing are Bird's-nest ferns (*Asplenium nidus*), clumps of Ixora, Hibiscus and more recently, Heliconia. None of these last three is native to Borneo but all add to the natural attraction of the hot springs for nectar-loving birds as well as for the myriad butterflies such as the magnificent black and yellow *Troides* birdwings, among many others, which come to sip the mineral rich waters.

Many butterflies can be seen in the small but well-maintained enclosed butterfly farm in which about 60 species, including Rajah Brooke's Birdwing are bred. The farm was opened to the public in 1995 and on a sunny day black-and-yellow birdwings, smoky blue-black mormons, black, white and red swallowtails, brown autumn-leaves and white orange-tips are all common in the clearing. Rajah Brooke's Birdwing is also seen here quite often. In the enclosure food plants for the caterpillars and flowering shrubs are grown. Extra food is also provided for the butterflies in the form of honey-water and juicy fruit. Eggs are searched for regularly and when found are removed for protection to a separate breeding house. When the adult butterflies emerge they are released back into the enclosure. Thus, unlike any other farm of this kind, all the butterflies are bred locally, rather than collected from outside, so that the wild populations are not depleted. There is also a small exhibit centre here.

The Hot Springs themselves, trickles of steaming water bubbling up from under large boulders, were first discovered by the Japanese during WW II, but the Park did not start any development until 1966. The hot sulphur water has now been piped into a series of functional, rather than aesthetic, open Japanese style tiled bath-tubs set in a natural clearing with many picnic shelters. Secluded bath cabins for those who want more privacy are also available at extra cost. Cold water swimming pools make a refreshing change.

Sitting in the pools at night, under the stars, watching a Colugo glide across the clearing was often a highlight of earlier visits, as was watching groups of hornbills flighting across the clearing in the early morning. Such sights are not common now but in the early morning and evening when few people are around, the pools clearing can still be rewarding in terms of wildlife.

The beautiful black and russet-red Prevost's Squirrel can often be seen feeding in the trees, together with little tree-shrews scampering up and down lianas. On the lowland forest fringe you might see a slender green vine snake (*Ahaetulla* sp.) or the bright green tree lizard *Bronchocoela cristatella*, which, like the tree-frogs, is capable of changing its colour to suit its background, while fatter but just as sleekly sinuous racer snakes (*Elaphe* spp.) may glide silently through a bamboo clump.

Small flying lizards of the genus *Draco* sometimes glide across the clearing. These lizards are most active in the early part of the morning, the males often flashing bright yellow or orange dewlaps on their throats to warn rivals away from their territory. Flying frogs and flying snakes are also recorded from Poring.

When launching itself from a tall tree-top, a flying snake can flatten its body, trapping a pocket of air underneath to slow its writhing descent to a tree as much as fifty metres (yards) away. The flying lizards of the genus *Draco* can extend the ends of their ribs, which are covered in a loose flap of skin, to form stiff "wings", when they jump, while Borneo's flying gecko and flying frogs have extensive webbing between their long fingers and toes and flaps of skin along their bodies that act like small parachutes.

Flying squirrels include the largest gliding creatures in the world and it is not unusual for them to cover more than 100 metres (yards) in a single glide. The larger flying squirrels, about the size of small cat, have furred flaps of skin (called a patagium) along their sides stretched between their arms and legs so they look almost like furry kites when they glide, using their long flattened tails as rudders to pull themselves steeply up and back before landing. They spend the hot daylight hours resting in the tree holes, becoming active at dusk, when they have occasionally been seen gliding across the hot pools clearing.

The flying lemur or Colugo (which is not a lemur at all) is about the same size but looks more like a large parachute in flight with even its tail enclosed in the patagium, thus easily distinguishing it from the squirrels. Like the

*Flying Squirrel*

## Flying creatures

Nowhere outside S.E.Asia do you find so many species of "flying" creatures – snakes, lizards and frogs as well as several species of flying squirrels and the flying "lemur" or Colugo. Of course, these animals do not really fly, but the ability to glide makes it easier to escape predators and to travel through the forest in search of food without having to descend to the ground. In Borneo the huge stature of the lowland dipterocarp forest is unmatched, and thus it is that in these forests development of animals that "fly" has reached its peak, using the immense height of the trees to glide great distances.

squirrels it is nocturnal, resting clinging to tree trunks or under big branches during the day – it has sometimes been seen along the Langanan waterfall trail in this position.

For birdwatchers, Poring is one of the best places in Sabah for lowland to hill forest birds. Typical lowland forest species of drongos, leafbirds, malkohas, woodpeckers, broadbills and the lovely Asian Fairy Bluebird are all common as well as more urban species such as the Yellow-vented Bulbul and the Magpie Robin. The gorgeous Black and Red Broadbill with its startling blue bill, characteristic of forest rivers, is common here. Along more undisturbed forest streams black and white Chestnut-naped Forktails flit from boulder to boulder, while along quieter parts of the trail the occasional pitta might be seen looking for insects. Poring is also a particularly good place for sunbirds and spiderhunters who frequent the clumps of flowering gingers and introduced Heliconias, in search of both nectar and insects. At least seven of the ten Borneo sunbirds are recorded from Poring and six of the seven Borneo spiderhunters.

### CANOPY WALKWAY

Beyond the pools lies the forest. Many of the dipterocarps in the lowland forest reach a height of 60 metres (200 feet) or more, but even higher stand the emergents, at 70 – 80 metres (230 – 260 feet). Though several dipterocarps do emerge above the main canopy, the tallest trees are the *menggaris* or *kayu rajah* (*Koompasia excelsa*) in the bean family, characterised by their smooth silvery-grey trunks and wide spreading crowns of delicate feathery foliage.

*Menggaris* trees are the kings of the forest but the tree is rarely felled, for its timber is brittle and the trunk is so smooth and hard that even the Honey Bear cannot climb it. Perhaps this is why the *menggaris* is the favourite home of another of Borneo's honey bees, the giant *Apis dorsata*, which builds its heavy combs weighing as much as 20 kilograms (45 pounds) or more under the branches, a veritable banquet for Honey Bears, if only they could reach them. *Apis dorsata* do not build permanent nests, but follow the flowering trees. They will come back to the same site every year if conditions are favourable. Recent research conducted at the Lagud Sebrang research station has discovered that these bees forage for nectar only on bright, moonlit nights, and that the reason they build their combs high up could be partly so that they can see their way home in the dim moonlight, as the hanging combs will be silhouetted against the sky.

The bears may not be able to climb the *menggaris* trees, but in more urban areas even the *dorsata* bees cannot escape the ingenuity of man who builds flimsy ladders of rattan and bamboo, climbing in the night with smoky torches to raid for honey.

The lowland dipterocarp forest at Poring has developed on relatively poor soils in hilly terrain and thus does not reach its maximum height here, but the *menggaris* trees still stand head and shoulders above the rest.

A few minutes walk into the forest will bring you to the entrance of the path up to the Canopy walkway. This is not for those who suffer from real vertigo, but Park staff are on hand to help those who are merely nervous. Visitors who do reach the canopy are rewarded with an experience of the forest treetops that is hard to forget. It is best to leave early, as soon as the walkway opens at 0700, as big tour groups often turn up after 1000.

The winding path, zig-zagging up a ridge from the entrance gate, where you pay your fee, takes about 20 minutes. It is fairly steep and slippery in wet weather so good footwear is essential. The shallow valleys are filled with thorny rattan palms, and fallen leaves and sometimes fruits of the giant forest dipterocarps litter the path, their trunks soaring high above. If you stand at the base of one of these giant dipterocarps at the side of the path, and look up the impressive bole which soars clear for 20–30 m (65–100 feet) before the first branches, only then do you appreciate the immensity and age of these forest giants. High on the branches are large epiphytic nest ferns that would not fit into an ordinary car. Notice also how the neighbouring tree crowns of these giants do not overlap or merge into one another – a distinct phenomenon known as 'tree shyness'. The word "dipterocarp" comes from the Latin, meaning "two-winged fruit", and nearly all dipterocarp fruits bear these wings, though they may be three, or even five in number. At the top of the path, at the base of the tower leading up to the walkway, are several clumps of giant bamboos.

The walkway consists of four sections made from single planks laid on aluminium ladders with rope handrails and netting to prevent accidents. In total it is over 157 metres (515 feet) long and 41 metres (135 feet) high at its highest point. It is basically built in the shape of a "T", the left arm being much longer than the right. The first section, the vertical part of the "T", ends at a magnificent *menggaris* tree around which a broad wooden platform has been built just below the branches.

Here, high in the canopy, a myriad species live out their lives without ever touching the ground. Flowering tree crowns and climbers are attended by a host of insects and birds, and breezes constantly rustle the leaves.

From here, the right hand arm of the "T" gives access to some good views looking east over the forest canopy to disturbed land and forest outside the Park. Trees of a small-fruited wild durian, *Durio griffithii*, grow here, with tiny spiny red fruits, only about five centimetres (2 inches) long. These split open on the tree to reveal the black seeds covered by a thin dry red aril inside which is particularly attractive to squirrels and hornbills. Other fruit trees that can be seen from the walkway include a wild mango and a small fruited species of *Artocarpus* as well as the much larger fruited *tarap*. *Aglaia* trees here bear long strings of dirty-white fruits, rather like those of the Langsat, hanging from the trunk. The left hand arm continues on to a second superb *menggaris*.

Just before this tree is reached, a magnificent giant Snake Orchid, *Grammatophyllum kinabaluensis,* can be seen in another tree close to the walkway – a huge epiphytic clump at least five metres (16 feet) across, with long snaky stems up to three metres (10 feet) in length. The Snake Orchid flowers rarely, but in full bloom it is a magnificent sight, its two metre (six feet) tall spikes covered in the spotted yellow-brown flowers that have given it its other name, the Tiger Orchid, though this name may also refer to the tiger-stripe pattern of leaflets on the stem. This orchid is one of the world's largest in terms of mass and a spectacular sight in flower. Its spiny roots point upward to trap leaf litter, forming its own personal compost heap.

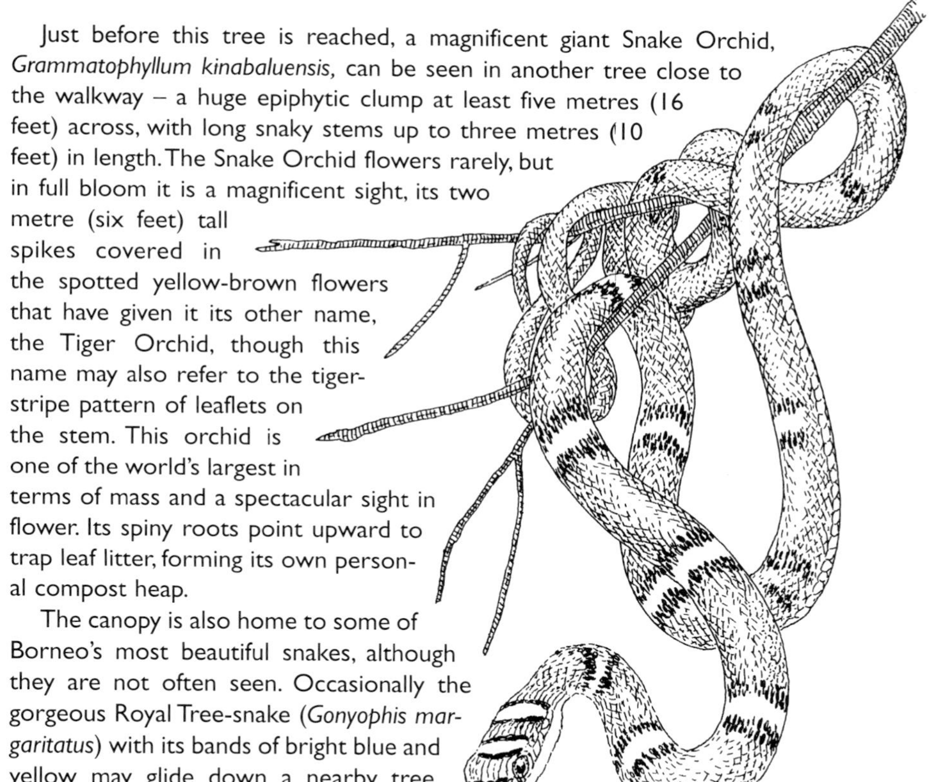

Flying Snake

The canopy is also home to some of Borneo's most beautiful snakes, although they are not often seen. Occasionally the gorgeous Royal Tree-snake (*Gonyophis margaritatus*) with its bands of bright blue and yellow may glide down a nearby tree trunk. Other tree snakes sometimes seen along the Canopy walkway are so-called "flying" snakes of the genus *Chrysopelea*, including the rare and beautiful Twin-barred Tree Snake (*Chrysopelea pelias*) and the Paradise Tree Snake (*Chrysopelea paradisi).* For all these the canopy is their true home and they are rarely seen near the ground.

The trail down from the other end of the canopy walkway follows another ridge with a beautiful stream and waterfall that provide the high humidity which encourages a luxuriant growth of ground herbs, wild gingers, ferns and aroids.

## KIPUNGIT WATERFALL AND LANGANAN WATERFALL

The start of this trail is the same as that to the Canopy walkway but turns to the right before reaching the entrance to the Canopy walkway path.

The forest here is rich in fruit trees. Some labelled trees that surround the pool clearing and which grow at the start of the trail include the wild *Artocarpus* species *tarap* and *togop* as well as langsat and rambutan. Other distinctive trees at the forest edge here are the *binuang* (*Octomeles sumatrana*) with its tall silver trunk and open crown of scattered large, often rather moth-eaten leaves, and the *pangi* (*Pangium edule*), a much neater tree with its compact crown of dark green heart-shaped leaves. The fruits of the *pangi* are quite unusual, large, round and heavy like

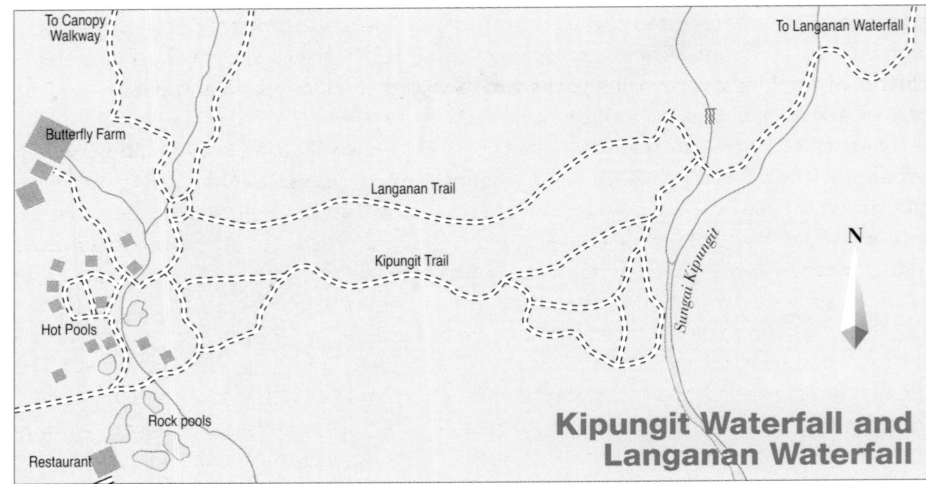


cannon-balls, the inside filled with a mass of triangular seeds all fitting together like a jigsaw puzzle. These seeds are sometimes seen for sale in more rural markets and are used by the Dusun people to preserve meat, though they can be poisonous if not treated properly.

The Kipungit waterfall is only a fifteen minute stroll. The path continues straight and flat before climbing the side of a cleared hill, covered in secondary vegetation, old tapioca plantings and a few remnant trees including one stately *binuang*. Small trees of *Macaranga*, typical components of secondary forest, grow in the sunshine at the edge of the path – some of these may have nests of scurrying, biting black ants living in the hollow stems.

At the top of the hill the trail enters the forest again. Other ants seen in the forest proper include the solitary giant *Campanotus gigas*, about 2.5 centimetres (1 inch) long, that scurries busily here and there along the trail. Although it is always seen singly along the trails during the day, these ants can be found foraging in the canopy at night.

Less than five minutes later the upper part of the Kipungit waterfall is reached, broad rather than tall, it tumbles only 10 metres (30 feet) or so. The water in the stream below the falls is shallow and cold and makes a refreshing dip for those returning from the longer trek to the Langanan waterfall.

Shelters and picnic tables have been set up at the base of the Kipungit waterfall and further down the stream near an open grassy clearing. Public toilets have also been built here. The Kipungit stream rushes and tumbles over boulders, its banks overhung with ferns and gingers, here and there bypassing a shallower calm pool where it is possible to paddle. One can return to the hot pools clearing along a level lower path with thick stands of gingers and palms growing in the forest.

From the upper path the Langanan Waterfall Trail leads steeply upwards to the Langanan waterfall. After crossing the Kipungit stream (be prepared to either take shoes and socks off or to get wet feet if there has been a lot of rain) it immediately starts to climb the forested slopes on the other side, still dominated by dipterocarps and fruit trees. About 90 minutes of fairly steep climb brings you to the Bat caves, a cluster of tumbled overhanging rocks with a strong smell of guano and tales of snakes as well as the bats which fly out in a panic if disturbed.

Leeches still occur at this lower level in the park, so leech socks should be worn, especially in wet weather. Both the common lowland forest leeches are found here: the Brown Leech whose bite is painless and which lives among the leaf litter on the ground, and the Tiger Leech that has a bright green or yellow stripe along its side. The Tiger Leech is more likely to hang on to tips of leaves overhanging the path, and its bite can sting as it injects no anaesthetic, unlike its brown cousin.

More welcome animals often seen along the path are the forest millipedes. There are two common species here – the long Black Millipede up to 30 centimetres (12 inches) in length and the short fat Pill Millipede only about 8 centimetres (3 inches) long. Both curl up into balls when disturbed but if left for a few seconds they will normally uncurl and allow visitors to watch them go about their business.

Skink lizards may skitter across the rustling leaves and occasionally the Horned Frog, one of Kinabalu's most unusual species, may be seen. It is camouflaged to resemble the dead leaves of the forest floor among which it lives, even to the extent of having flaps of skin (the "horns") projecting over the eyes and nose, and ridges of skin along the back that look like the veins of leaves. The loud honking sound of this frog before a storm is said to be one of the characteristic sounds of the lowland forest in the late afternoon or evening.

If you are really lucky you might encounter a small "dragon", one of the forest monitor lizards (*Varanus* spp), sunning itself at the edge of a trail. These species are related to the giant Komodo Dragon of Indonesia, and the most common is the *biawak* that is found in many suburban towns, as well as around Kampung Poring in swampy fields and drains. The *biawak*, which does not reach much more than a metre (three feet) in length, will not be seen along the trail. The forest species are generally larger, reaching a length of nearly two metres (six feet), and though they look ungainly, they can climb trees with great agility and speed when disturbed.

Further up at a steep corner in the path was the only site known in the Park for the elusive *Rhizanthes* – a parasitic flower related to *Rafflesia* but one which is much rarer and is far less studied. The flowers of *Rhizanthes* are much smaller than *Rafflesia*, reaching only 20 centimetres (8 inches) or so across with up to 16 long thin petals, tapering into mere filaments at their tips. Unfortunately work on the path some years ago appears to have destroyed the site, but *Rhizanthes* could occur elsewhere along this path.

Still higher up the forest begins to change. First fallen acorns litter the path as oaks and chestnuts begin to dominate. Dipterocarps are now almost gone but here and there the beautiful soaring trunks of the hill and cloud dipterocarps can be seen, and their winged fruits too will cover the trail in season – these trees are the last outpost of the great dipterocarp clan that once reigned throughout the lowland forests.

As the path grows steeper, the forest changes yet again, where a band of ultramafic soil crosses the path. Now the forest is more open and the fallen spiky seed capsules of the Mountain Casuarina, *Gymnostoma (Casuarina) sumatrana,* lie on the path together with its fine needle-like foliage. Conifers also appear, their lacy crowns seen silhouetted through gaps in the canopy on the ridge top as the mountain breezes whisper soft, now loud, through their fine feathery foliage.

At last the faint murmur of the falls can be heard above the wind in the canopy, the trees open out and there is the Langanan waterfall, a torrent of frothy white water tumbling more than 30 metres (100 feet), to the dark moss-covered boulders around the pool at the base with a sparkling spray covering the sides of the waterfall, edged with bright green aroids and ferns growing in the perpetual damp.

When the Poring station first opened, walking the Langanan Waterfall Trail almost guaranteed sightings of larger mammals such as the Orang-utan, or a sign of its presence in the form of old 'nests' in which the Orang-utan sleeps, building a new one from interlaced branches in the treetops every night. Such a sighting would be rare nowadays, but deer and Wild Pig are recorded regularly along here together with both the Pig-tailed Macaque and the Maroon Langur. The Langanan Waterfall Trail is also still good for birdwatching, though the calls of the Argus Pheasant resounding through the forest and of hornbills overhead that were once common are now rare.

Of the other primates, only two of Borneo's five species of langur or leaf-monkey have been recorded from the park. Both are endemic to the island. The Grey Langur, a lowland species, is found only in north and north-eastern Borneo, mainly in primary forests, while the Maroon Langur occurs across the island in lowland and hill forests and up to 3,000 metres (9,850 feet) in the montane forests of Kinabalu. Both species travel mainly in small family groups of six to eight and are active during the day, feeding on young leaves and seeds.

The Bornean Gibbon, another endemic, found in lowland primary forest up to 1,500 metres (4,900 feet) has also been recorded from Poring as have Borneo's only two nocturnal primates – the teddy-bear-like Slow Loris and the bug-eyed Western Tarsier. While the Bornean Gibbon also travels in small family groups of three to five, both the Slow Loris and the Tarsier tend to lead more solitary lives, often in the denser old secondary forests, feeding on insects.

*Pig-tailed Macaque*

# SAYAP

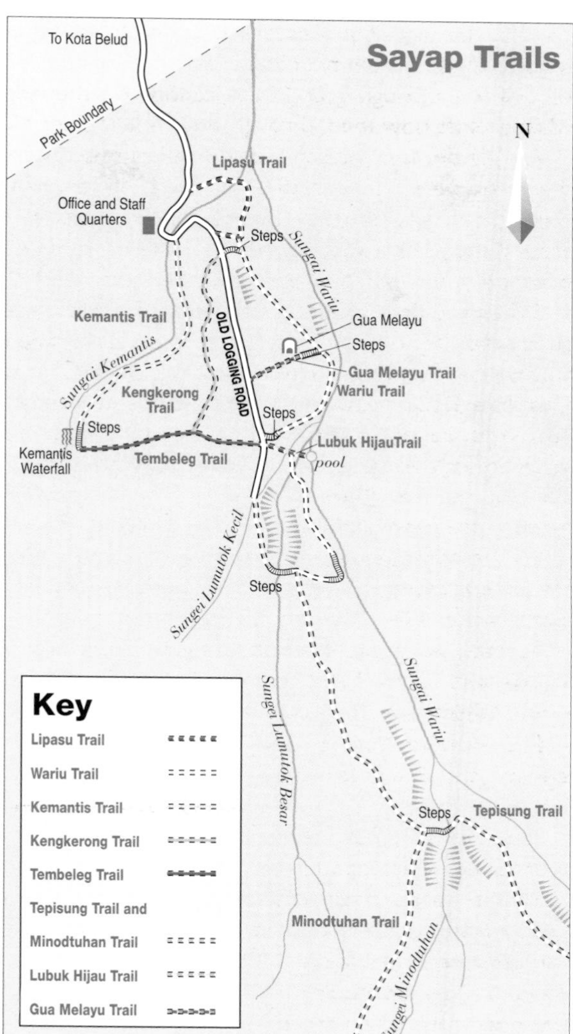


Set at an elevation of about 1,067 metres (3,489 feet) on the west side of Kinabalu, the sub-ranger station of Sayap is often called "the other side of the mountain". The main aim of the station, which was established in 1991, was to control illegal logging and hunting on the western boundary – mute evidence of the former can be seen in the remains of an old logging road that pushes a kilometre (less than a mile) or so into the Park from the station and is now the starting point for many trails.

### THE ROAD TO SAYAP.

Sayap lies about two hours drive from Kota Kinabalu in good weather with a four wheel drive vehicle. To reach it one must first drive north to the small rural town of Kota Belud, by-passing the town of Tuaran with its colourful Sunday *tamu* or market, to cross the wide, muddy Tuaran river which offers wonderful views of the mountain from its banks. Beyond the river, the road passes along the new coastal highway through a patchwork of rubber-clad low hills and rice fields on the right and heavily disturbed mangrove forest on the left, with the occasional old fruit garden full of mango trees. After about 15 minutes the road crosses the Sulaiman river which empties into the huge mangrove inlet of Tasik Sulaiman. Just beyond are the old shophouses of Tenghilan and as the road then rises there is a superb view of Kinabalu in good weather. Above the patchwork of hills and fields, the mountain stands clear, with no electricity poles or wires to bar the view, its long eastern ridge running down to the left. It is another 15-20 minutes to Kota Belud.

The Bajau people who live in the Kota Belud area are famed for their horses and it is not unusual to see ponies being ridden along the grassy roadside verges. Kota Belud is a good place to stop for coffee and the fried Indian pancake, *roti canai*, eaten with or without an egg in a local coffee shop. It is also the last place to buy petrol or diesel and any other basic supplies.

Once refreshed follow the left hand road out of town to Kudat and Kota Marudu, past the mosque, crossing the wide sluggish Tempasuk river with spreading rain trees along its banks, and more views of the mountain before coming to a little roundabout. Here visitors to Sayap take the right hand turn to 'Kem Paradise', the army camp. From here the road leads through the camp and on into the foothills.

There are signs to Sayap at all the junctions but some are small and easy to miss so drive slowly. Buffaloes are a common sight and once past the army camp, the government cattle farm on the right is an excellent place to see egrets perched on the backs of cows or following them through the grass. The road becomes a narrow gravelled track leading through rubber plantations and pineapple farms, narrowing valleys and ever more precipitous slopes with wonderful views of the mountain peaks.

About 30 kilometres (19 miles) from Kota Belud, the little *kampung* of Sayap is reached at an elevation of about 1,000m (3,270 feet), with colourful flowers planted round the houses and fruit trees growing everywhere. Even the steepest hillsides here are cultivated with pineapples and hill rice, and on the small flat patches on the valley floors, wet rice is grown on tiny terraces.

Six km (four miles) beyond Kampung Sayap the Park boundary is reached and the vegetation changes abruptly, the road now lined with forest trees for the last few minutes drive to the Sayap station on the Kemantis stream above the Wariu river. The station consists only of a small office and quarters for the Park staff where the road stops and there is nowhere for visitors to stay overnight unless they bring tents and their own camping equipment. Nevertheless the area is popular as a picnic spot, particularly at weekends and on public holidays. During the week, however, it is practically deserted, which adds much to its charm.

Sayap's elevation means that the vegetation here is mainly hill-dipterocarp forest with a fair scattering of oaks, chestnuts and figs. The commonest families are the Euphorbiaceae and the Annonaceae, often cauliflorous, with flowers and fruit carried on the trunk. The Annonaceae is the family to which both the temperate Custard Apple and tropical Soursop fruits belong. Plants in this family are easily recognised by their curious fleshy three-petalled flowers. Bunches of the distinctive red or pinky-purple flowers of *Goniothalamus* in this family are often seen strung low down around the base of the trunk. The fruits of *Goniothalamus* are not considered edible, but some are said to have medicinal uses. Occasional fruit trees such as wild mangosteen, durian and *pangi* also occur. Aroids, ferns, gingers and other herbaceous plants are also common in the humid riverbank environment.

Bird and butterfly watching are both rewarding pastimes at Sayap, though the mammal life is poor – probably a result of illegal hunting in the past by people living outside the boundary, exacerbated by the increased access afforded by the old logging road. Although the Mountain Tree-shrew is quite common, so far the only published record of anything larger is that of a Barking Deer in 1995, and about the

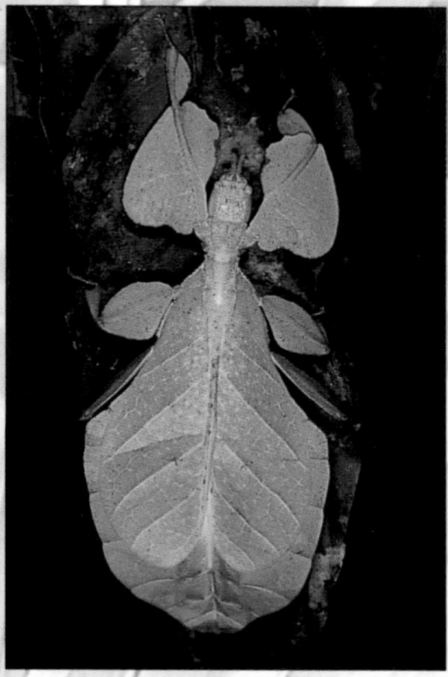

ABOVE: THE LEAF INSECT IS A MASTERPIECE OF NATURAL MIMICRY.

RIGHT: THE STRIKING ASIAN FAIRY BLUEBIRD IS ONE OF THE CHARACTERISTIC BIRDS OF THE LOWLAND FOREST.

BELOW: THE MOUNTAIN'S TREASURE-TROVE OF ORCHID DIVERSITY INCLUDES SLIPPER ORCHIDS (LEFT) AND BULBOPHYLUM ORCHIDS (RIGHT).

LEFT: TWISTING GIANT LIANAS ARE A FEATURE OF LOWLAND MIXED DIPTEROCARP FOREST.

BELOW: RAJAH BROOKE'S BIRDWING IS ONE OF THE LARGEST AND MOST SPECTACULAR BUTTERFLIES TO BE SEEN AT PORING HOT SPRINGS.

OPPOSITE ABOVE: THE NOCTURNAL TARSIER USES ITS AMAZING AGILITY TO CATCH AND EAT LARGE INSECTS IN THE FOREST CANOPY .

OPPOSITE BELOW: THE RAFFLESIA, THE WORLD'S LARGEST FLOWER, IS FOUND NEAR PORING, BUT HAS PROVED NOTORIOUSLY DIFFICULT TO CULTIVATE.

THE MESILAU RESORT IS DOMINATED BY THE JAGGED PEAKS OF THE MESILAU PINNACLES.

largest animals easily seen are large black millipedes which can sometimes be found along trails. The bird life is a mix of montane species near the lower limit of their range, with some lowland birds reaching their upper limits. The montane treepies, drongos, Laughing-thrushes and yuhinas are common, together with the Indigo Flycatcher and the Snowy-browed Flycatcher. Other montane forest residents include the elusive Whitehead's Trogon and shy Whitehead's Broadbill as well as the two montane partridges and the Golden-naped Barbet. But lowland species of barbets, woodpeckers, and leafbirds have all been recorded, as well as the ubiquitous Yellow-vented Bulbul and the Bushy-crested Hornbill. Published studies on the bird life are few and although there are only 52 species presently recorded for Sayap, this is certainly more a reflection of the lack of observation than the lack of bird life, which is both rich and varied.

*Golden-naped Barbet*

The abandoned logging road crosses the Kemantis stream by a small ford and continues for about 1 kilometre (over half a mile) into the Park along a flat, gently ascending terrace above the Wariu river. This terrain is part of the former Wariu Valley, when it was about 200m (650 feet) wider than it is today. Glacial erosion may be responsible for the huge amount of sedimentary rocks and gravel that now fills the former valley and which forms the wide flat terraces that make walking the trails here so enjoyable. Below, the river flows swiftly through a steep sided valley filled with large mossy boulders. A well developed trail network has been established around the station and the Wariu river, many of the trails starting from this abandoned road. All trails are well signposted and times given allow for fairly leisurely walking, but some of the descents to the Wariu river are extremely steep.

**Kemantis Trail** (30 minutes)

This trail starts on the other side of the Kemantis stream at the station. It is an easy walk, following the Kemantis stream up to the Kemantis waterfall. A steep 5 minute ascent up the hill at the side of the waterfall brings you to the Tembeleg Trail at the top of the waterfall. On a sunny morning, sparkling rainbows can often be seen at the viewpoint here between 0800 and 1000.

## Strangling fig

A strangling fig starts life as a seed dropped by a pigeon or a hornbill high in a forest tree. Slowly the fig sends down thin, tendril-like roots,reaching for the ground and puts forth green leaves to the sun. Once the roots reach the ground they thicken, and as they thicken they squeeze the host trunk, gradually constricting its food and water supply. So the host tree slowly starves to death and the trunk decays. The strangler lives on and continues to put down roots, eventually creating a forest of trunks supporting its massive leafy crown, and providing a banquet of fruit for birds and other animals which disperse the seeds.

**Tembeleg Trail** (50 minutes)

The entrance to the Tembeleg Trail is about 25 minutes along the logging road opposite the entrance to the Lubuk Hijau Trail. It crosses the flat riverine terraces high above the Wariu to the right of the old logging road, before rising gently up the hillside right to the top of the Kemantis waterfall.

**Kengkerong Trail** (30 minutes)

This trail starts 4 minutes along the old logging road, close to the entrance to the Wariu trail opposite, and runs across the extensive river terraces to meet the Tembeleg trail about halfway along as it starts to rise.

**Lubuk Hijau Trail** (40 minutes)

The entrance to the trail is about 30 minutes along the old logging road, opposite the Tembeleg trail on the other side. From here it is a very steep 5 minute descent to the river bank and another 5 minutes winding through large mossy boulders to reach Lubuk Hijau or the "green pool". The pool lies on the boulder-strewn Wariu river at the base of a large smooth rock over which the icy mountain waters pour milky white into the pool below. The banks are lined with mossy boulders, interspersed with small trees and many shade and damp-loving herbaceous flowers.

**Minodtuhan Trail/Tepisung Trail**

The Minodtuhan Trail leads upstream for an hour or so from Lubuk Hijau to the Minodtuhan stream near the junction with the Wariu. Here the trail forks, the right following the Minodtuhan stream, while the left (the Tepisung trail) follows the Wariu through a sunken valley rich in herbaceous flowers, ferns and epiphytes that lies along an ancient fault plane.

**Gua Melayu Trail** (25 minutes)
The entrance to the trail lies 20 minutes along the old logging road. Gua Melayu or "Malay Cave" itself, lies a few minutes from the entrance of the trail at the top of the steep descent to the Wariu river. Like most of Kinabalu's so-called "caves" Gua Melayu is nothing more than a large overhanging rock set in a clump of bamboos. In the past it has been used as a shelter by hunters.

*Rhinoceros Hornbill*

**Wariu Trail** (45 minutes to Lubuk Hijau)
This trail starts only 4 minutes along the old logging road opposite the Kengkerong Trail, descending immediately to the Wariu river and following its course upstream to Lubuk Hijau. A magnificent Strangling Fig tree stands just inside the entrance at the top of the river bank, almost straddling the trail with its massive trunks. Orange-brown protective bracts, shed as the young shoots unfold their leaves, litter the old road beneath with every leaf flush.

**Lipasu trail** (30 minutes)
The trail starts only 2 minutes along the old logging road, following the Wariu downstream and joining the main Sayap road just before it reaches Sayap station.

# SERINSIM

The sub-ranger station of Serinsim, in the lowlands, lies at an elevation of only 152m (500 feet) on the Park's north-eastern boundary. Like the Sayap station, the Serinsim station was set up to control illegal logging incursions into the Kinabalu Park and there are few visitor facilities. It is only a few kilometres from Poring Hot Springs as the crow flies; to get there, however, is a long journey from Kota Kinabalu, through Kota Belud, round the top of the Park, passing through Kota Marudu and back down the eastern side. This takes at least three and a half hours, longer in wet weather, and a four-wheel drive vehicle is essential.

## THE ROAD TO SERINSIM

The first part of the road is the same as that leading to Sayap, but at the little round-

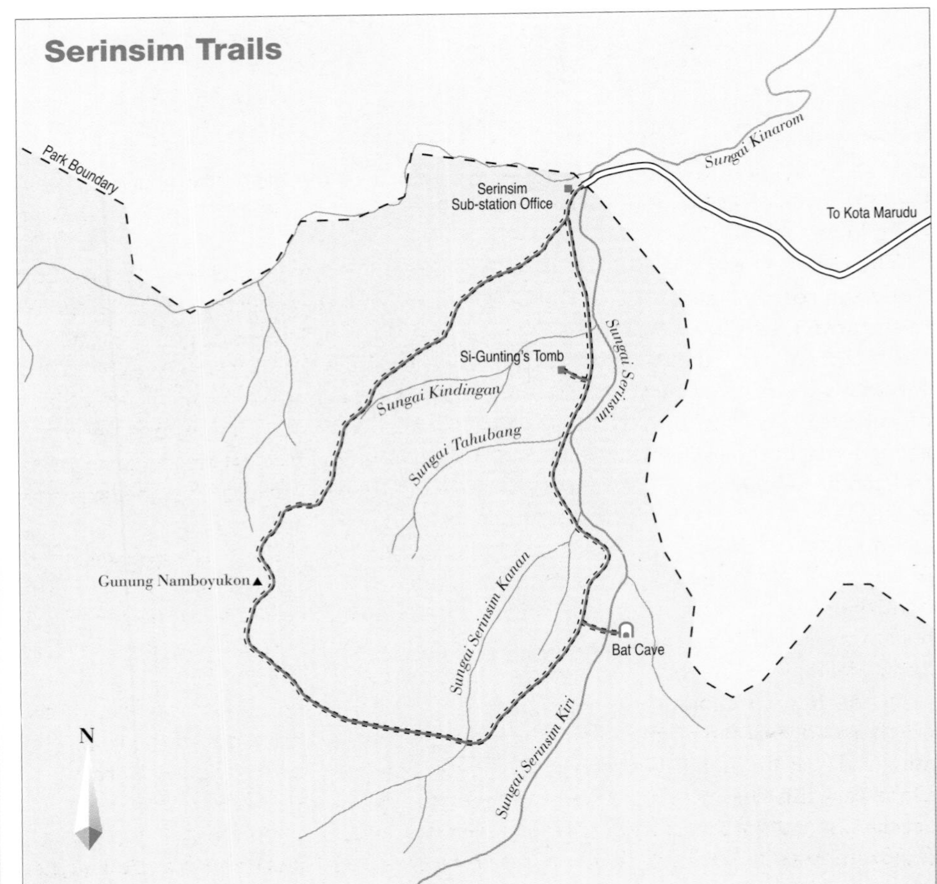

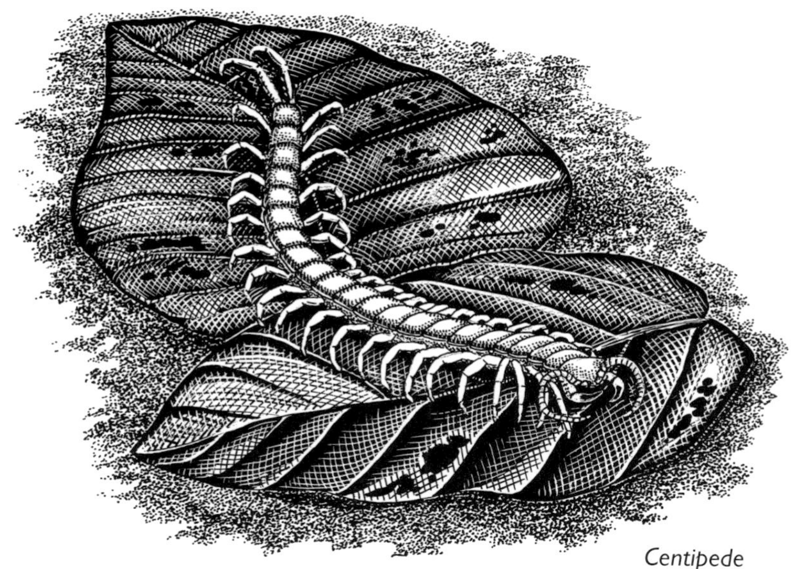

*Centipede*

about just beyond Kota Belud, visitors to Sayap take the right hand turn to 'Kem Paradise', while Serinsim travellers keep left along the road to Kudat and Kota Marudu.

The road is sealed all the way to Kota Marudu. About 15 minutes after leaving Kota Belud the road, which has been following a small winding tributary of the Tempasuk river, turns north across the wide, flat, Tempasuk plain, with the mountain and its foothills dominating the view to the right. On the left the plain stretches down to the sea with wide shallow inlets and low sandy dunes with coconut groves behind. Much of this area is part of the Kota Belud Bird Sanctuary which is home to many interesting birds, both resident and winter visitors. Large flocks of egrets live in the area and can be seen in small "V" formations, flying across the road to their night roosts at dusk.

Every now and then a spreading rain-tree at the edge of the road shades a group of lazy cows – a definite road hazard to be watched for if travelling at dusk. On the right the plain is covered with rice fields right up to the foothills with the occasional buffalo, attended by an egret or two. Cattle egrets habitually stay close to these large beasts, feeding on the insects and other small creatures disturbed by their grazing.

In another 15 minutes or so you reach the small *kampung* of Pendasan at the northern edge of the plain. Huge old fruit trees grow on both sides of the road, creating a dim leafy tunnel, with the crystal-clear Pendasan stream rippling through it. Once past this charming spot roadside vegetation gives way to secondary scrub and acacias as the road turns towards the hills with the low peaks of Langui-Langui (1,201 metres/3,930 feet), Templar (1,137 metres/3,720 feet) and Madalon (1,121 metres/3,667 feet), bordering the road on the right. These hills are all within the

## What's in a name?

Gunung Tamboyukon is the name generally given to the large peak standing between Mount Kinabalu and Serinsim, while the very similar Gunung Namboyukon refers to the smaller sharp peak directly above Serinsim station. There is controversy over these names however. Some, particularly the people of Kampung Serinsim, say that the smaller peak should rightfully be called Tamboyukon. Until this is resolved, we prefer to use the accepted park nomenclature, but anyone visiting Serinsim should be aware of this problem.

northern extension of the Kinabalu Park, but were much burnt along their slopes during the 1998 drought.

Soon, passing over a low ridge, past *kampungs* selling baskets and fruits, the road follows the valley of the Mengaris river down to the flat coastal plain, where ranks of oil palm dominate the scene. Here it divides sharply, the left junction leading to Kudat and the right on to Kota Marudu, first through oil palms and then through ricefields with the large-leaved fan-palm *Corypha*, appearing amidst the rice. This unusual palm produces one huge, immensely striking, branched head of tiny flowers before it dies. Even if none of the palms are in flower, a dead one, its leaves already fallen, but with the remains of its huge inflorescence silhouetted against the sky can often be seen. The local people here call it *tukar*, and use its huge leaves to thatch temporary shelters. On through the padi-fields, groves of coconuts and old fruit gardens to a large bridge just before Kota Marudu town. Cross the bridge and continue straight on at the small roundabout, before turning left down Jalan Cempaka to the new township. This is the last place before Serinsim to stock up on basic essentials, petrol or diesel.

The turn off to Serinsim is located on the right hand side of the road at Jalan Lotung, just in front of the ESSO petrol station, before the Jalan Cempaka turn off to the town.

From here, the road heads towards the hills. It is only another 38 kilometres (24 miles) to Serinsim but the road is very rough save for the first 6 kilometres (4 miles), and takes well over an hour, more in wet weather.

Occasional lovely views of the flat open plain stretching down to Marudu bay, fringed with mangrove and with the hills of Kudat beyond can be seen. The vegetation along the road itself is mainly secondary scrub, much of which has been repeatedly burnt when cleared for shifting cultivation decades ago. Fires during the El Nino drought in 1998 also burnt large parts of the Kinabalu Park here.

About halfway to Serinsim, if the weather is clear, impressive views of the northern end of the Park and Gunung Tambuyokon appear, with the small, pointed, triangular peak of Gunung Nambuyokon (1,681metres/5,515feet) sticking sharply up above both the *kampung* and the station of Serinsim. Kampung Marak-Parak is passed and then the village of Serinsim is soon reached. Here it is necessary to ford four small streams before reaching Serinsim station itself, only five minutes beyond the *kampung*.

## SERINSIM AND ITS TRAILS.

Because Serinsim was set up to control illegal logging there are few visitor facilities. The station is set at the junction of the Kinarom and the Serinsim rivers and provides a delightful area for picnics at the edge of the wide, shallow Kinarom river, fringed with orange-flowering *Saraca* trees. Public showers and toilets have been provided and camping is permitted here for those who wish to stay overnight – bring your own tents, food and equipment.

Two trails have been developed but they are quite rough, especially in wet weather and bridges across small streams consist merely of notched logs. The trails pass through burnt-out secondary forest dominated by bananas for at least the first 30-40 minutes. These bananas and other secondary shrubs cut out any breezes and it is relief to reach unburned forest at last.

Both trails start at the same place behind the station at the edge of the burnt forest, but after about 10 minutes the track divides, the right hand section leading up to the summit of Gunung Namboyukon; the left hand one to the Bat Cave. Times given on the sign-board at the entrance are for the very fit and about half the time again should be allowed for those who wish to walk more slowly.

### Bat Cave and Si-Gunting's tomb.

The Bat Cave trail takes about three hours. The trail is mostly flat to undulating, following a low terrace above the Serinsim river for much of its route and crossing some pretty streams, as well as several minor rivulets. Indeed in several places, the rivulets run down the trail, making for muddy walking in wet weather.

The first 30 minutes leads through burnt secondary forest, until the Kindingan river is reached. The fires were not able to cross this stream and the forest beyond, though

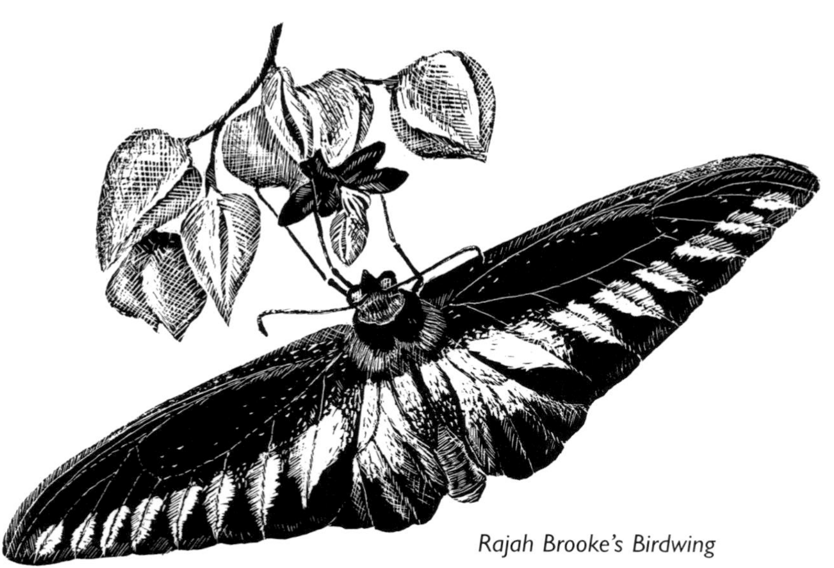

*Rajah Brooke's Birdwing*

still old secondary, is much cooler, with taller trees and a fairly open undergrowth. Leeches are scarce, a reflection of the lack of mammals in the area, but forest millipedes are common later in the day. Nearer the Bat Caves, in taller forest, birdwatching is said to be good. Huge fallen leaves on the path are those of *tarap* and *togop* (*Artocarpus* spp), while large shiny round brown beans along the path belong to the *merbau*, (*Intsia palembanica)*, which produces a lovely timber.

Another ten minutes or so, brings you to the tomb of Panglima Si-Gunting, a Dusun warrior hero who fought a seven year guerilla war against British rule from 1894 to 1901. Si-Gunting was born in Serinsim, and died there at the age of 47, a few years after peace had been declared. His tomb is set on a small hill above the trail, on land that was farmed by his ancestors more than a century ago.

From here it is about another two and a half hours to the Bat Cave. The trail continues along the terraces above the Serinsim river, crossing the Tahubang river. An old landslide between this and the next stream, the Serinsim Kanan, involves a rather steep detour, very slippery in wet weather. There is another climb before crossing the Serinsim Kiri, just below the Bat Cave, set in a steep rock face above the stream. The entrance, about 5 metres (16 feet) above the ground, is reached by a steep iron ladder. Once through the low mouth, the cave inside soars high above, the ceiling lined with hundreds of bats.

**Gunung Nambuyukon Summit Trail**

The Gunung Namboyukon trail used to continue from the Bat Cave, but involved two nights camping on the trail and so is now largely abandoned. Another, shorter, trail leads up a closer, steeper ridge but even this is said to take four and a half hours up and and the same coming back down. This is a relatively recent trail, and apart from the park staff who actually cut the trail, the only people who have walked it have been – to our knowledge – a few particularly enthusiastic botanists. We have not climbed it ourselves and those who wish to try either route to the summit of Namboyukon should consult the park authorities first and arrange for a guide. A description of this trail should be sought from park authorities. The first hour or so of walking however, passes through burnt out secondary forest and bananas, rough, steep and overgrown to the base of the mountain, at a place known as Bee rock, where *Apis dorsata* bees have built their combs under rock ledges.

# Address Book

**Sabah Parks**
Lot 3, Block K
Sinsuran Complex
88000 Kota Kinabalu
Sabah, Malaysia.
PO Box 10626
88806 Kota Kinabalu
Sabah, Malaysia
Tel: (088) 211 881
Fax: (088) 221 001

**Kinabalu Nature Resort Sdn. Bhd.**
Lots 3.46 and 3.47, 3rd fl. Bl. C
Karamunsing Complex
88300 Kota Kinabalu
Tel: (088) 243 629
Fax: (088) 242861
email: nature@kinabalu.net
Website: http://www.nature.kinabalu.net/

**Sabah Tourism Promotion Corporation**
No. 51 Jalan Gaya
88000 Kota Kinabalu
Sabah, Malaysia.
Mail Bag 112
88999 Kota Kinabalu
Sabah, Malaysia
Tel: (088) 212 121
Fax: (088) 212 075/219 311
email: sabah@po.jaring.my
Website: http://www.jaring.my/sabah

**WWF Malaysia (Sabah Office)**
Suite 1 – 6 W11, 6th Floor CPS Tower
1 Jalan Centrepoint
88800 Kota Kinabalu
Sabah, Malaysia
Tel: (088) 262 420
Fax: (088) 242 531

**Sabah Sports and Recreation Society** and **Sabah Mountain-Biking Association**
c/o Dato Dr. Hashim A. Wahab
(President)
Promenade Hotel
No. 4, Lrg. Api-Api: Api-Api Centre
88000 Kota Kinabalu
Tel: (088) 265555
Fax: (088) 257348.
email: hasbaw@pc.jaring.my

**The Sabah Society,**
Lot 39-1, 1st Fl, Damai Plaza Phase IV
Luyang, Kota Kinabalu.
PO Box 10547
88806 Kota Kinabalu
Sabah, Malaysia
Tel/fax: (088) 250443
email: sabsoc@po.jaring.my
Website: http://www.sbs-online.com/sabahsociety/

**Borneo Magazine**
C/o Borneo Travel News Sdn. Bhd.
3rd Fl; Lot B; Block A;
Damai Commercial Centre Phase IV
Tel: (088) 264401
Fax: (088) 259516
email: brmag@tm.net.my

**NB The international dialling prefix for Malaysia is 60. When calling from outside the country, delete the first 0 from the local code.**

# References and Further Reading

Books listed here include reference material as well as less specialised and more historic texts.

Argent, C., A. Lamb, A. Phillipps and S. Collenette. 1988. *Rhododendrons of Sabah.* Sabah Parks, Kota Kinabalu.

Briggs, John. 1988. *Mountains of Malaysia: a Practical Guide and Manual.* Longman Malaysia.

Beaman, John H and Reed S. 1988. *The Plants of Mount Kinabalu. Vol. 3. Gymnosperms and non-orchid monocotyledons.* Natural History Publications (Borneo) in association with the Royal Botanic Gardens, Kew, UK.

Burbidge, F.W. 1880. *Gardens of the Sun.* John Murray, London.

Campbell, Elaine J.F. 1994. *A walk through the Lowland Rain Forest of Sabah.* Natural History Publications in association with Borneo Rainforest Lodge, Kota Kinabalu.

Chan, C.L., A.Lamb, P.S.Shim and J.J.Wood. 1994. *Orchids of Borneo. Vol. 1. Introduction and a Selection of Species.* Sabah Society in association with the Royal Botanic Gardens, Kew, UK.

Clarke, Charles. 1997. *Nepenthes of Borneo.* Natural History Publications, Kota Kinabalu in association with Science and Technology Unit, Sabah.

Cribb, Phillip. 1997 *Slipper Orchids of Borneo.* Natural History Publications.

Davison, G and Gerald Cubitt. 1999. *The National Parks and other Wild Places of Malaysia.* New Holland Publishers, London.

Davison, G.W.H. and Chew Yen Fook. 1998. *A Photographic Guide to the Birds of Borneo.* New Holland Publishers, London.

Frahm, Jan Peter, Wolfgang Frey, Harald Kurschner and Mario Menzel. 1996. *Mosses and Liverworts of Mount Kinabalu.* Natural History Publications in association with Sabah Parks Trustees, Kota Kinabalu.

Ghazally Ismail and Laily bin Din (eds). 1995. *A Scientific Journey through Borneo: Sayap-Kinabalu Park Expedition.* Pelanduk Publications, Kuala Lumpur.

Inger, R.F. and F. L. Tan. 1996. *The Natural History of Amphibians and Reptiles.* Natural History Publications.

Inger, Robert F. and Robert B. Steubing. 1997. *A Field Guide to the Frogs of Borneo.* Natural History Publications in association with Science and Technology Unit, Sabah.

Kamaruddin Mat Salleh. 1991. *Rafflesia – Magnificent Flower of Sabah.* Borneo Publishing Company, Kota Kinabalu.

Mackinnon, John and Karen Phillipps. 1993. *A Field Guide to the Birds of Borneo, Sumatra, Java and Bali.* Oxford University Press.

Parris, B.S., R.S. Beaman and J. H. Beaman, 1992. *The Plants of Mount Kinabalu, Volume I: Ferns and fern allies*. Royal Botanic Gardens, Kew, UK.

Payne, Junaidi, Gerald Cubitt, Dennis Lau and Jayl Langur. 1999: *This is Borneo – Sabah, Sarawak, Brunei and Kalimantan.* New Holland Publishers London

Payne, Junaidi. Charles M. Francis and Karen Phillipps. 1985. *A Field Guide to the Mammals of Borneo.* Sabah Society.

Pegler, David N. *The Larger Fungi of Borneo.* 1997. Natural History Publications.

Phillipps, Anthea and Anthony Lamb. 1996. *Pitcher-plants of Borneo.* Natural History Publications, Kota Kinabalu.

Phillipps, Susan M. 1995. *Enchanted Gardens of Kinabalu: A Borneo Diary.* Natural History Publications.

Robson, Craig. *Field Guide to the Birds of South-east Asia.* New Holland Publishers, London. The most recent field guide, covering all 1,250 birds found on mainland South-east Asia – including many species also found on Borneo and Indonesia.

Seow-Choen, Francis. 1997. *A Guide to the Stick and Leaf Insects of Singapore.* Singapore Science Centre, Singapore.

Smythies, Bertram E. 1999. *Birds of Borneo*, 4th ed revised. Natural History Publications (Borneo), in asscociation with the Sabah Society, Kota Kinabalu.

St. John, Spenser. 1862. *Life in the Forests of the Far East.* 2 volumes. Smith Elder and Co., London.

Steubing, Robert B and Robert F. Inger. 1999. *A Field Guide to the Snakes of Borneo.* Natural History Publications (Borneo).

Vermeulen, J.J. 1991. *Orchids of Borneo. Vol. 2. Bulbophyllum.* Bentham-Moxon Trust, Royal Botanic Gardens, Kew and Toihaan Publishing Company, Kota Kinabalu in association with the Sabah Society, Kota Kinabalu.

Whitehead, J. 1893. *The Exploration of Kina Balu, North Borneo.* Gurney and Jackson, London.

Wood, J.J. 1997. *Orchids of Borneo. Vol. 3. Dendrobium, Dendrochilum and others.* The Sabah Society in association with the Royal Botanic Gardens, Kew, UK.

Wood, J.J., R.S. Beaman and J.H. Beaman. 1993. *The Plants of Mount Kinabalu. Vol. 2: Orchids.* Royal Botanic Gardens, Kew, UK.

Wong, K.M. and A. Phillipps (eds). 1996. *Kinabalu: Summit of Borneo*, revised and expanded edition. The Sabah Society in association with the Sabah Parks, Kota Kinabalu.

Wong, K.M. and C.L. Chan. 1997. *Mount Kinabalu: Borneo's Magic Mountain.* Natural History Publications, Kota Kinabalu.

In addition, articles in the following journals are a source of much information.

*Sabah Society Journal*, Kota Kinabalu

*Sabah Parks Journal*, Kota Kinabalu.

*Borneo Magazine*, Kota Kinabalu

# Checklist of Birds of Kinabalu Park

- ❑ Little Heron
- ❑ Storm's Stork
- ❑ Bat Hawk
- ❑ Crested Honey Buzzard
- ❑ Brahminy Kite
- ❑ Chinese Goshawk
- ❑ Crested Goshawk
- ❑ Japanese Sparrowhawk
- ❑ Besra
- ❑ Grey-faced Buzzard
- ❑ Changeable Hawk Eagle
- ❑ Blyth's Hawk Eagle
- ❑ Rufous-bellied Eagle
- ❑ Black Eagle
- ❑ Mountain Serpent Eagle
- ❑ Crested Serpent Eagle
- ❑ White-fronted Falconet
- ❑ Peregrine Falcon
- ❑ Oriental Hobby
- ❑ Eurasian Kestrel
- ❑ Blue-breasted Quail
- ❑ Red-breasted Partridge
- ❑ Crested Partridge
- ❑ Crimson-headed Partridge
- ❑ Great Argus
- ❑ Red-legged Crake
- ❑ White-breasted Waterhen
- ❑ Common Sandpiper
- ❑ Pintail Snipe
- ❑ Thick-billed Pigeon
- ❑ Little Green Pigeon
- ❑ Pink-necked Pigeon
- ❑ Jambu Fruit Dove
- ❑ Green Imperial Pigeon
- ❑ Mountain Imperial Pigeon
- ❑ Ruddy Cuckoo Dove
- ❑ Little Cuckoo Dove
- ❑ Spotted Dove
- ❑ Emerald Dove
- ❑ Blue-crowned Hanging Parrot
- ❑ Large Hawk Cuckoo
- ❑ Hodgson's Hawk Cuckoo
- ❑ Moustached Hawk Cuckoo
- ❑ Indian Cuckoo
- ❑ Oriental Cuckoo
- ❑ Banded Bay Cuckoo
- ❑ Plaintive Cuckoo
- ❑ Rusty-breasted Cuckoo
- ❑ Violet Cuckoo
- ❑ Little Bronze Cuckoo
- ❑ Gould's Bronze Cuckoo
- ❑ Drongo Cuckoo
- ❑ Common Koel
- ❑ Raffles's Malkoha
- ❑ Black-bellied Malkoha
- ❑ Chestnut-bellied Malkoha
- ❑ Red-billed Malkoha
- ❑ Chestnut-breasted Malkoha
- ❑ Greater Coucal
- ❑ Lesser Coucal
- ❑ Reddish Scops Owl
- ❑ Mountain Scops Owl
- ❑ Collared Scops Owl
- ❑ Rajah's Scops Owl
- ❑ Barred Eagle Owl
- ❑ Collared Owlet
- ❑ Brown Hawk Owl
- ❑ Short-tailed Frogmouth
- ❑ Javan Frogmouth
- ❑ Malaysian Eared Nightjar
- ❑ Large-tailed Nightjar
- ❑ Grey Nightjar
- ❑ White-nest Swiftlet
- ❑ White-bellied Swiftlet
- ❑ Brown Needletail
- ❑ Silver-rumped Spinetail
- ❑ Asian Palm Swift
- ❑ Whiskered Treeswift
- ❑ Grey-rumped Treeswift
- ❑ Diard's Trogon
- ❑ Red-naped Trogon
- ❑ Whitehead's Trogon
- ❑ Scarlet-rumped Trogon
- ❑ Cinnamon-rumped Trogon
- ❑ Orange-breasted Trogon
- ❑ Banded Kingfisher
- ❑ Rufous-collared Kingfisher
- ❑ Collared Kingfisher
- ❑ Black-capped Kingfisher
- ❑ Blue-banded Kingfisher
- ❑ Oriental Dwarf Kingfisher
- ❑ Blue-throated Bee-eater
- ❑ Red-bearded Bee-eater
- ❑ Dollarbird
- ❑ Bushy-crested Hornbill
- ❑ Wreathed Hornbill
- ❑ Black Hornbill
- ❑ Pied Hornbill
- ❑ Rhinoceros Hornbill
- ❑ Helmeted Hornbill
- ❑ Malaysian Honeyguide
- ❑ Brown Barbet
- ❑ Gold-whiskered Barbet
- ❑ Red-crowned Barbet
- ❑ Red-throated Barbet
- ❑ Yellow-crowned Barbet
- ❑ Golden-naped Barbet
- ❑ Mountain Barbet
- ❑ Black-throated (Bornean) Barbet
- ❑ Blue-eared Barbet
- ❑ Rufous Piculet
- ❑ Crimson-winged Woodpecker
- ❑ Checker-throated Woodpecker
- ❑ Banded Woodpecker
- ❑ Rufous Woodpecker
- ❑ Grey-capped Woodpecker
- ❑ Buff-rumped Woodpecker
- ❑ Buff-necked Woodpecker
- ❑ Grey-and-Buff Woodpecker
- ❑ Olive-backed Woodpecker
- ❑ Maroon Woodpecker
- ❑ Orange-backed Woodpecker
- ❑ Green Broadbill
- ❑ Hose's Broadbill
- ❑ Whitehead's Broadbill
- ❑ Long-tailed Broadbill
- ❑ Black-and-Red Broadbill
- ❑ Black-and-Yellow Broadbill
- ❑ Banded Broadbill
- ❑ Dusky Broadbill
- ❑ Blue-banded Pitta
- ❑ Blue-headed Pitta
- ❑ Banded Pitta
- ❑ Blue-winged Pitta
- ❑ Asian House Martin
- ❑ Pacific Swallow
- ❑ Barn Swallow
- ❑ Grey Wagtail
- ❑ Forest Wagtail
- ❑ Large Woodshrike
- ❑ Bar-bellied Cuckoo-shrike
- ❑ Black-faced Cuckoo-shrike
- ❑ Lesser Cuckoo-shrike
- ❑ Black-winged Flycatcher-shrike
- ❑ Bar-winged Flycatcher-shrike
- ❑ Grey-chinned Minivet
- ❑ Fiery Minivet
- ❑ Scarlet Minivet
- ❑ Brown Shrike
- ❑ Tiger Shrike
- ❑ White-breasted Wood Swallow
- ❑ Common Iora

- ❑ Lesser Green Leafbird
- ❑ Greater Green Leafbird
- ❑ Blue-winged Leafbird
- ❑ Asian Fairy Bluebird
- ❑ Black-and-White Bulbul
- ❑ Black-headed Bulbul
- ❑ Black-crested Bulbul
- ❑ Scaly-breasted Bulbul
- ❑ Straw-headed Bulbul
- ❑ Flavescent Bulbul
- ❑ Yellow-vented Bulbul
- ❑ Olive-winged Bulbul
- ❑ Red-eyed Bulbul
- ❑ Cream-vented Bulbul
- ❑ Spectacled Bulbul
- ❑ Grey-cheeked Bulbul
- ❑ Ochraceous Bulbul
- ❑ Yellow-bellied Bulbul
- ❑ Hairy-backed Bulbul
- ❑ Streaked Bulbul
- ❑ Ashy Bulbul
- ❑ Siberian Blue Robin
- ❑ Pied Chat
- ❑ White-browed Shortwing
- ❑ Oriental Magpie Robin
- ❑ White-crowned Shama
- ❑ White-crowned Forktail
- ❑ Chestnut-naped Forktail
- ❑ Blue Rock Thrush
- ❑ Mountain Blackbird
- ❑ Eyebrowed Thrush
- ❑ Orange-headed Thrush
- ❑ Everett's Thrush
- ❑ Chestnut-capped Thrush
- ❑ Sunda Whistling Thrush
- ❑ Black-breasted Fruithunter
- ❑ Malaysian Rail Babbler
- ❑ Black-capped Babbler
- ❑ Temminck's Babbler
- ❑ Short-tailed Babbler
- ❑ White-chested Babbler
- ❑ Ferruginous Babbler
- ❑ Horsfield's Babbler
- ❑ Rufous-crowned Babbler
- ❑ Scaly-crowned Babbler
- ❑ Moustached Babbler
- ❑ Sooty-capped Babbler
- ❑ Chestnut-backed Scimitar Babbler
- ❑ Striped Wren Babbler
- ❑ Mountain Wren Babbler
- ❑ Eyebrowed Wren Babbler
- ❑ Striped Tit-babbler
- ❑ Fluffy-backed Tit-babbler
- ❑ Grey-throated Babbler
- ❑ Grey-headed Babbler
- ❑ Black-throated Babbler
- ❑ Chestnut-rumped Babbler
- ❑ Chestnut-winged Babbler
- ❑ Rufous-fronted Babbler
- ❑ Black Laughing-thrush
- ❑ Sunda Laughing-thrush
- ❑ Chestnut-capped Laughing-thrush
- ❑ White-browed Shrike Babbler
- ❑ Brown Fulvetta
- ❑ Chestnut-crested Yuhina
- ❑ White-bellied Yuhina
- ❑ Golden-breasted Gerygone
- ❑ Bornean Stubtail
- ❑ Sunda Bush Warbler
- ❑ Kinabalu Friendly Warbler
- ❑ Yellow-bellied Prinia
- ❑ Middendorff's Warbler
- ❑ Arctic Warbler
- ❑ Mountain Leaf Warbler
- ❑ Yellow-breasted Warbler
- ❑ Yellow-bellied Warbler
- ❑ Mountain Tailorbird
- ❑ Rufous-tailed Tailorbird
- ❑ Ashy Tailorbird
- ❑ White-throated Fantail
- ❑ Spotted Fantail
- ❑ Pied Fantail
- ❑ Grey-headed Flycatcher
- ❑ Dark-sided Flycatcher
- ❑ Ferruginous Flycatcher
- ❑ Asian Brown Flycatcher
- ❑ Verditer Flycatcher
- ❑ Indigo Flycatcher
- ❑ Blue-and-White Flycatcher
- ❑ White-tailed Flycatcher
- ❑ Malaysian Blue Flycatcher
- ❑ Hill Blue Flycatcher
- ❑ Bornean Blue Flycatcher
- ❑ Snowy-browed Flycatcher
- ❑ Mugimaki Flycatcher
- ❑ Rufous-chested Flycatcher
- ❑ Narcissus Flycatcher
- ❑ Little Pied Flycatcher
- ❑ Pygmy Blue Flycatcher
- ❑ Fulvous-chested Jungle Flycatcher
- ❑ Grey-chested Jungle Flycatcher
- ❑ Rufous-tailed Jungle Flycatcher
- ❑ Eyebrowed Jungle Flycatcher
- ❑ Rufous-winged Monarch
- ❑ Maroon-breasted Monarch
- ❑ Asian Paradise Flycatcher
- ❑ Japanese Paradise Flycatcher
- ❑ Bornean Mountain Whistler
- ❑ Velvet-fronted Nuthatch
- ❑ Yellow-rumped Flowerpecker
- ❑ Yellow-breasted Flowerpecker
- ❑ Yellow-vented Flowerpecker
- ❑ Plain Flowerpecker
- ❑ Black-sided Flowerpecker
- ❑ Scarlet-backed Flowerpecker
- ❑ Orange-bellied Flowerpecker
- ❑ Plain Sunbird
- ❑ Brown-throated Sunbird
- ❑ Red-throated Sunbird
- ❑ Ruby-cheeked Sunbird
- ❑ Purple-naped Sunbird
- ❑ Purple-throated Sunbird
- ❑ Olive-backed Sunbird
- ❑ Crimson Sunbird
- ❑ Scarlet Sunbird
- ❑ Little Spiderhunter
- ❑ Long-billed Spiderhunter
- ❑ Spectacled Spiderhunter
- ❑ Yellow-eared Spiderhunter
- ❑ Grey-breasted Spiderhunter
- ❑ Streaky-breasted Spiderhunter
- ❑ Whitehead's Spiderhunter
- ❑ Black-capped White-eye
- ❑ Everett's White-eye
- ❑ Pygmy White-eye
- ❑ Mountain Blackeye
- ❑ Asian Glossy Starling
- ❑ Pin-tailed Parrotfinch
- ❑ Tawny-breasted Parrotfinch
- ❑ Dusky Munia
- ❑ Black-headed Munia
- ❑ Crow-billed Drongo
- ❑ Ashy Drongo
- ❑ Bronzed Drongo
- ❑ Hair-crested Drongo
- ❑ Greater Racket-tailed Drongo
- ❑ Black-naped Oriole
- ❑ Dark-throated Oriole
- ❑ Black-and-Crimson Oriole
- ❑ Crested Jay
- ❑ Common Green Magpie
- ❑ Short-tailed Green Magpie
- ❑ Bornean Treepie
- ❑ Black Magpie
- ❑ Large-billed Crow
- ❑ Slender-billed Crow

# Language

Visitors to Kinabalu may find the following local words or phrases useful.

**Air:** water
**Berapa:** how?
**Berapa jauh:** how far?
**Berapa ringgit:** how much?
**Berat:** heavy
**Binatang:** animal
**Bising:** noise
**Boleh:** can
**Bunga:** flower
**Burung:** bird
**Binuang:** the forest tree *Octomeles sumatrana*
**Cepat:** fast
**Daun:** leaf
**Dekat:** near
**Gunung (G):** mountain
**Hujan:** rain
**Ikan:** fish
**Jaga:** be careful
**Jalan:** path
**Jalan kaki:** walk
**Jalan raya:** road
**Jam:** hour
**Jangan:** don't
**Jatu:** fall
**Jauh:** far
**Katak:** frog
**Kampung (kg):** village
**Kayu rajah:** the forest tree *Koompasia excelsa*
**Licin:** slippery
**Makan:** eat
**Minum:** drink
**Menggaris:** the forest tree *Koompasia excelsa*
**Merbau:** the timber tree *Intsia palembanica*
**Naik:** up, go up
**Pacat:** leech
**Panas:** hot
**Panat:** tired
**Pelahan-pelahan:** slow
**Pokok:** tree
**Pangi:** the forest tree *Pangium edule*
**Pisang:** banana
**Pisang hijau:** green banana
**Pisang mas:** golden banana
**Pisang merah:** red banana
**Pondok:** a small shelter
**Rehat:** rest
**Sakit:** sick
**Sakit kepala:** headache
**Sana:** there
**Sini:** here
**Sejuk:** cold
**Sungei:** river
**Tidak:** no, not
**Tidak apa:** never mind
**Tidak boleh:** cannot
**Tunggu:** wait
**Terjun:** waterfall
**Turun:** down, descend
**Tamu**: open-air market
**Tarap:** the fruit tree *Artocarpus odoratissimus*
**Togop:** the bark cloth tree *Artocarpus elasticus*
**Tuhau:** a wild ginger, *Etlingera punicea*
**Tukar:** the fan-leaved palm *Corypha elata*
**Ular:** snake

***Numbers***

**Satu:** one
**Dua:** two
**Tiga:** three
**Empat:** four
**Lima:** five
**Enam:** six
**Tujoh:** seven
**Lapan:** eight
**Sembilan:** nine
**Sepuluh:** ten

# Index